NOTHING WASTED

LEARNING TO BELIEVE YOU ARE ENOUGH IN A WORLD OF LABELS

by Randy Rich

with Stephen Copeland
foreword by Mike Novak

PRAISE FOR
NOTHING WASTED

"The greatest lesson I've learned in following Christ is that Jesus didn't save me to live for Him; Jesus saved me so that He could live through me! And that is not just semantics, it is the difference between religion and relationship. This basic understanding of identity in Christ goes by many names: the Christ-life, living grace, the abundant life, the abiding life, etc. But regardless of what it's called, it is rooted in the reality that who I am is who I am in Christ. In his new book, *Nothing Wasted*, my friend Randy Rich explores the riches of this identity in Christ and demonstrates what it looks like to live this out in your everyday life."

Vance Pitman, Senior Pastor, Hope Church Las Vegas

"Knowing Randy since we were both in our young twenties, he has been a dear friend, Denver Bronco teammate, and fellow brother in Christ. I wholeheartedly encourage you to read *Nothing Wasted* and go on this journey with Randy to see what treasures God will awaken in you. This book will inspire and help you find your true identity in a supernatural God who knew you before the foundations of the world—how that relationship will transform your life. Through Randy's transparency in revealing his struggles, you will come face-to-face with whatever labels the enemy has put on you through your friends, family, coaches, or even yourself—the labels that rob, steal, and destroy the very best things that God has destined you to walk in. Don't miss this opportunity to examine the pain, shame, and guilt that needs to be put in its proper place in order to live out the calling that God has for each of us."

Steve Foley, Denver Broncos defensive back (1976–1986),
all-time interception leader

"Through my relationship with Randy Rich, I have always seen how much he cares about people. A godly and energetic man, his enthusiasm and willingness to reach out to others with words of hope and encouragement is unparalleled. From his help raising funds for children's causes by participating in our Jelly Belly Celebrity Charity Golf tournaments, to his work with teens in his Dare to Dream school assembly programs, his passion for encouraging others to realize their value and worth through the Lord's eyes shines brightly. In his book, *Nothing Wasted*, he sheds light on the important yet painful task of self-evaluation and the shedding of negative labels that are applied to us by helping us realize the grace and love that God has for us. His vulnerability in sharing his life story and intense desire for us to learn from his mistakes is truly a blessing.

Lisa Rowland Brasher, President & CEO, Jelly Belly Candy Co.

"I first met Randy Rich in 1978 when he became a teammate of mine on the Cleveland Browns. Randy and I immediately connected as we shared a like belief and commitment of our lives to Jesus Christ. I was touched by his faith, humility, and hunger to know God's Word. I had no idea of the hurt and shame Randy harbored within. The truth revealed, at times we all hide our mistakes, anxieties, worries, fears, and self-doubts. Read Randy's story. I believe it will help you to take a look into your own heart and awaken you to the reality that you are God's precious and special child. God, the Creator of the universe, loves you. No one on earth can replace you."

Don Cockroft, Cleveland Browns punter-kicker (1967–1980), Author of The 1980 Kardiac Kids: Our Untold Stories

"You really get to know a guy when you travel around the world with him. Few people I've known have had the tenacity and *can-do* attitude of Randy Rich! After following him into the jungles of Africa, through the poverty-stricken streets of India, and around the endless sea of faces in China, I realized that this was a special individual. Driven by his undying love of God and life, and his heart for people, Randy will captivate you with his dynamic personality—and his book will do the same. I am proud to call him a friend."

JD Chandler, on-air personality and deejay, K-LOVE Radio

"I have known Randy Rich for a long time. We met through playing with the Denver Broncos. Randy was truly a God-send in my life, and we still have a great friendship today. In 1977 Randy helped the Broncos reach their first Super Bowl, which was Super Bowl XII. It was an honor to have played with him. Randy has always been a good, honest, and caring man and friend. He is a loving man who lives according to his faith. I know his book will be inspiring to anyone who struggles with their own life situations."
__Rick Upchurch, Denver Broncos wide receiver (1975–1983), four-time Pro Bowler__

"Randy has incredible and infectious energy. The way he inspires those who know him and those who meet him is through his animated communication, filled with both humility and courage. This book quickly captures his spirit as it draws the reader in so deeply and purposefully to the beautiful message of self-worth and becoming everything you dream of. (God doesn't make mistakes!) Randy effectively shares his story with such impact that one is left hopeful and confident."
__Gia Kramer, President, Quality Property Management__

"I had the privilege to coach Randy Rich when I was the head coach of the Cleveland Browns. My coaching career revealed an important truth that talent is God-given but character is a matter of choice. Randy Rich is the rare individual who possesses both. His book speaks to his remarkable talent and character."
__Sam Rutigliano, Cleveland Browns head coach (1978–1984)__

"I've known Randy for years. He was, at one time, a development officer for International Cooperating Ministries. He was ambitious and energetic—eager to fulfill God's purpose for his life. He always wore his Super Bowl ring—very thankful for the time he spent in the NFL—and to talk to him, I had to peek around that gigantic ring! In all seriousness, he never bragged about his past accomplishments. The more I talked with Randy, the more I discovered his deep love and devotion to Christ. I know you will be blessed by his book."
__Dois Rosser, Founder and Chair Emeritus, International Cooperating Ministries__

"My credentials for offering this endorsement? Fifty-five years, during which I have experienced every aspect of life with this man. Friendship, love, anger, hurt feelings, pain, but most importantly: Christ Jesus and Him crucified for our sins. In Randy's book, you will be enriched, educated, and edified. You will learn what it means to never give up and to never succumb to the labels placed on you by others."

Bill Nichols, North High teammate and best friend

"Randy's story from growing up in Oildale, California, to making it to the Super Bowl with the Denver Broncos is inspiring! Seeing how Christ has worked in his life along the way will bring hope to every reader. It's a story that inspires you to make the most of your God-given talents and opportunities."

David Pierce, Chief Creative Officer,
K-LOVE Radio

"Randy came to the Denver Broncos midseason in 1977, filling a much-needed open position. His overachieving attitude fit in well with a team made up of a lot of overachievers. That '77 team was hungry for success and was comprised of a lot of really good people, so Randy fit into that culture perfectly. We nurtured the 'team' mentality, and every single guy on that team played a part in getting us to the Super Bowl. Randy made many lifelong friendships from his tenure with us, and I know those relationships formed the basis for him to live such a successful and fulfilling life. "

Red Miller, Denver Broncos head football coach
(1977–1980)

"Randy is a warrior. Against all odds on the football field—in high school, college and the NFL—his tenacious faith spurred his resiliency to overcome the labels others tried to put on him. As a business man, his faith continued to spark innovative approaches to enrich the lives of others. I walked with Randy as his faith and prayers formed Dare to Dream—a program that touches the lives of teens all over the country with a message of hope and inspiration. Dare to Dream transforms limitations and feelings of hopelessness into a world filled with possibilities. *Nothing Wasted* will do the same—helping you to surrender your weakness and insecurities to God so that He can turn them into strengths. Randy is an inspiring steward of His divine gifts; he leads by example and motivates others to be their very best."

Phil Bristol, Founder, President and CEO,
Projectivity Solutions

"The world would look at Randy, size him up, and label him as an underdog. And although Randy Rich's personal and professional career is packed full of outstanding highlights, he learned in his adult life what it meant to operate out of an understanding of who God is. This led Randy to know who he is as well. Nothing was impossible for God, and he lived out his life under this truth. Randy is one of the rare, genuine people that make you feel as though you have known him forever. It's his authenticity, gentleness, and humble spirit that makes him such a personal friend. Many might label him as an underdog, but Randy would only label himself as a child of God."

Scott Newton, Senior Pastor, Hope City North Carolina

"Randy Rich is an incredible communicator—with an amazing story to tell. He invites us into his story as a vehicle to explore our own journey. This book is a must-read for anyone who struggles to believe that he or she is enough in a confusing world that is full of comparisons and demands."

Chaz Corzine, Artist Manager, The Michael W. Smith Group

"I met Randy Rich at North Bakersfield High School. Coaches had told him that he was too small to play college football. But they didn't measure the size of his heart. He asked for a chance to prove himself. He more than proved himself. At New Mexico, he was a team leader, great safety, excellent punt returner, and a tough tackler. He was always an inspirational team member. I wasn't surprised when he played for the Denver Broncos and was on the field during the opening kickoff in Super Bowl XII. This book is an opportunity to get to know what is behind Randy's successes."

Bill Mondt, University of New Mexico Lobos head football coach
(1974–1979)

To my family and my wife.
All of you are echoes of God's grace in my life.

To Wayne Barber, the best mentor I ever had, who passed away while I was writing this book. You taught me of Living Grace, and I'll forever be learning about it.

To Turk Eliades, the best coach I ever had, who also passed away while I was writing this book.
You taught me to never give up.

And finally, to Mark and Gia Kramer.
Without your support, this book would not have been written.

TABLE OF CONTENTS

PART I: FOOTBALL - What Do You Do to Fill the Void?

PART II: LIFE - What Do You Do When the Cheering Stops?

FOREWORD
by Mike Novak, CEO at K-LOVE

I like to call Randy Rich my "2 a.m. friend." That's because if I ever need a listening ear—at any time of any day—I know that Randy will be there for me. To hear me. To help me. To encourage me. Having a friend like that, I've learned, is invaluable in life. He is truly one of the most loyal people you could ever meet.

I've known Randy for nearly two decades, and we have always had a lot in common. We are both "Valley Boys"—him having grown up in Bakersfield and me in Modesto, there in South Central California, back in the 1950s and '60s. We are both outdoorsmen—enjoying hunting and motorcycling together. And we have both always been drawn to contemporary Christian music and the impact that it can have on our culture and country.

Since hiring Randy at K-LOVE in 2010 to serve as our vice president of philanthropy, our relationship and brotherly bond has only grown stronger. We were even neighbors at one point, and he and his wife, Cathy, got married in my backyard. I feel like I've had the pleasure of having a front-row seat for his journey over the years—and especially since he moved to Sacramento to work at K-LOVE.

In many ways, Randy's new chapter in life, here in Sacramento, has given him an avenue to put into practice all the lessons he has learned over the years. It is a second chance for him. Another chance at marriage. Another chance to work in Christian music. Another chance to go around the country and share his story with students through our "Air1 Dare to Dream" school assemblies program. And it is a journey for him that is still unfolding. He is admittedly "in process."

Like most of our stories, Randy's is one of beauty, brokenness, and failures. The difference in Randy's story, however, is his approach. Whereas most of us try to hide the broken aspects of our stories, Randy is willing to vulnerably share his brokenness and mistakes with others—to relate to them, to let them know they are not alone, and to let them know that they are enough and that they are loved, no matter how they've been labeled and no matter what mistakes they have made.

That's exactly what Randy has done in his book, *Nothing Wasted: Learning to Believe You are Enough in a World of Labels.* His book is a real page-turner, and I read the entire manuscript in a week's time. It was an easy read but also a deep read, an emotional read but also an entertaining read. Overall, the lessons in his book were reminders to me to keep moving along, to keep trusting, to keep believing, and to continue to see what God has for me on my journey. I frequently found myself saying, "Me, too," as I read. It was no surprise to me that Randy's book was so relatable, as he is one of the most personable people I know.

I was moved and inspired in these ways while reading his book because there were a lot of different directions Randy could have gone in life. In his football career, he could have allowed the labels that others attached to him—that he was too small and too slow—to define him, but he didn't. In his mistakes, he could have allowed some of the labels that he put on himself out of his deep-seated sense of shame to define him, but he didn't. He could have allowed his insecurities to define him, but he didn't. He could have allowed his past to define him, but he didn't.

We all have areas in our lives in which we struggle to truly feel and believe that we are enough—whether it's in our faiths, relationships, careers, or pursuits. It's easy to sometimes believe the lie that God can't use us—that we are worthless—but *Nothing Wasted* is a manual for those who are tempted to believe those lies, which, on some level, is all of us.

One thing that impressed me with Randy in *Nothing Wasted* was his ability to be so deep and introspective. In many ways, it surprised me. I know Randy to be a very passionate, driven, and motivated man who is a natural leader and who is always trying to accomplish something. But I think that putting this book together forced him to slow down and evaluate some things in his life on a very deep level. In doing so, he challenges others to journey inward as well and to evaluate their own lives and decision-making. His book challenged me to do the same.

So what are the labels that you need to shed? How are others labeling you? How have you labeled yourself?

How would your life look if you chose to believe that—no matter

your successes or failures, no matter your past or present wilderness—
nothing in God's economy is wasted?

What if in your brokenness, you still dared to dream?

A NOTE TO THE READER
by Randy Rich

Who am I to write a book?

Though I had somewhat of a unique upbringing, it really wasn't that much different than many of my friends' childhoods. Though I had somewhat of a unique journey in the realm of football, my name will never be considered elite by any means—though I played with many elite players. And though I've had ups and downs in my personal life and professional life, doesn't *everyone* experience hardships?

I am nothing special (except to my friends and a few neighbors), but hopefully readers will be able to relate to the story and life of an average person like myself.

When I wrote *Nothing Wasted*, I was sixty-three years old. As you read, you will notice that I possess many stereotypical Baby Boomers traits. I am diligent, goal-oriented, self-assured, and competitive. I am a "doer" to a fault and an achiever. I have worked hard in my life, and I've enjoyed seeing the results of that hard work. I am part of a generation that seems to epitomize the values associated with the American Dream.

One of the dangers of being a doer, however, is that I rarely took time in my life to slow down and reflect. I rarely took the time to become aware of what was going on within me throughout life's circumstances, the good and the bad. On the outside, my life was marked by a solid work ethic and achievements, but inside, I was a chaotic mess. Some of this was the result of my unstable childhood and upbringing. Some of it was the result of my seemingly lifelong chase for approval and affection.

Whatever the case, I spent most of my life deeply insecure. I attempted to mask that insecurity through anger (a sure-fire way to take control of a situation) and through performance (either on the football field or in my job); both were ways that I flexed my strength. But the insecurities were always there.

When I became a Christian, the ideas of hope, eternity, and a sense of morality became important parts of my life, but I still was not an introspective person in the slightest. It really wasn't until my life began to fall apart—when my emotional sickness and my unease rose to the surface—that I was forced to become introspective. This caused me to transition into a new spiritual paradigm.

This book has taken that self-evaluation to another level. Writing *Nothing Wasted* was deeply painful. It was difficult to be vulnerable, honest, and open about my flaws and shortcomings. But readers will see that there is nothing wasted in God's economy—that's just how good He is and how incomprehensible His grace is.

And it is for this reason that I have chosen to delve into my failures—so that readers will not make the same mistakes that I did. If only I had been aware of my struggles within, then I would like to think that maybe I wouldn't have made some of the decisions that I made, which led to my life falling apart. If only I'd been as concerned about my internal battle as I'd been about my worldly journey—the hard work, the accomplishments, the status—then maybe my relationships with the people I love the most would not be so scarred today.

> *"The purpose of this book is to challenge readers to journey inward, as I journey inward, as well. Through sharing my story, I hope that readers will become aware of what is taking place beneath the surface of their lives as I share what was unfolding beneath the surface of my own."*

The purpose of this book is to challenge readers to journey inward, as I journey inward, as well. Through sharing my story, I hope that readers will become aware of what is taking place beneath the surface of their lives as I share what was unfolding beneath the surface of my own.

At times, this book is raw and dark and heavy. The purpose of this isn't to victimize myself or to "throw a pity party," as they say. Rather, I have intentionally ventured into these fragile, vulnerable places because seeing "the light at the end of the tunnel" often involves first having the courage to go through the lonely darkness of the tunnel. I've resolved that it would be wrong for me *not* to share what I've learned through the mistakes in my life with others, even if it is only a few readers.

At the end of each chapter is a section that consists mostly of my reflections, and in these "reflection sections" are statements that either read "I was unaware of…" or "I was beginning to understand…" These statements mirror the phrases "I was blind" and "Now I see"—the false self and the true self. We never reach the end of awareness. We never reach the end of seeing. Again, that's just how incomprehensible God's grace is.

In Part I, there are a lot of "I was unaware of…" statements. In Part II, there are a lot of "I was beginning to understand…" statements. Neither Part I or Part II is more important than the other, because, as you'll find out, these statements go hand-in-hand. For example, someone who is in an abusive relationship cannot begin to *understand* what a life with someone else might be like until the person becomes *aware* of the unhealthiness of the situation that he or she is in. Someone who focuses on improving the visible things on the outside, as I did, often either masks his or her internal insecurities or is entirely unaware of them.

When we are unaware, negative cycles form. When we become aware of what's happening at a deeper level—the level which God speaks to us, in that private sanctuary—we can create healthier cycles. And it has taken me a lifetime to learn that. For most of my life, I was afraid to venture into those unfamiliar, scary places within myself and bring resolve. And oh, by the way, please understand that at sixty-three years of age, I still have not arrived. I am still a work in progress.

Though the narrative in the manuscript covers several decades and a variety of different experiences in my life—sometimes unfolding slowly, sometimes unfolding rapidly—the reflection sections at the end of each chapter are the glue to the manuscript and are designed to suggest some insight that I have gained from my own spiritual journey. They are guideposts for spiritual growth and introspection. There are also discussion questions at the end of each chapter, in case you would like to take your processing and self-evaluation a step further with friends or family or in a small group at church.

Before you begin the first chapter, I would like to leave you with a quote from my late mentor Wayne Barber, who sadly passed away in September 2016. In his book *Living Daily in God's Grace*, Wayne writes: "He [God] is in the business of chipping away our exteriors so that the image of Christ can emerge."

That quote perfectly encapsulates this book.

Maybe *Nothing Wasted* can help you chip away your exterior as I continue to chip away my own.

I remember Wayne telling me many times, "Randy, you just need to let Jesus be Jesus in you."

Maybe this book can inspire you to let Jesus be Jesus in you, as I continue to do the same.

PART I:
FOOTBALL

What Do You Do to Fill the Void?

CHAPTER 1
The Other Side of the Tracks

I grew up with very few boundaries.

Little structure. No curfew. It wasn't uncommon for me or my five siblings to come through the doors of our home past midnight—even on school nights. How *could* there be structure? My parents were gone a lot. They were usually working. Not because they wanted to but because they *had* to so they could provide an average life for their kids.

If you lived as I did on the north side of the Kern River, which ran through Bakersfield, California, you were called a "River Rat"—a derogatory term in the day—by those who lived in Bakersfield. If you lived on the other side of the railroad tracks in Oildale, people saw you as a low-income, blue collar white person.

I grew up on the wrong side of the river on the wrong side of the tracks.

That's not to be hard on my family. I'm proud of where I was raised. Proud to be a "Dalian" (short for Oildalian). Proud to be an "08er" (short for 93308, Oildale's zip code). But it's also fair to say that my family fit the stereotypes of that day.

My father had a third-grade education. He was the main provider for my family, often working eighty to ninety hours a week as a truck driver. He was a rugged-looking man—about five feet eight inches with a pot belly from drinking beer and hard liquor. He had a hard life, and his body showed it.

At one point in my youth, Dad had the opportunity to acquire two trucking permits at a reasonable cost for the Central California area. Had he acquired them, Dad would have made money on the fees that truckers paid driving through Central California—kind of like a toll road fee collector. I'm told that this would have ultimately made him a millionaire.

But Dad decided not to acquire the permits. I'm told by my brothers that he was afraid of the paperwork. He didn't know how to read.

Mom had a high school education. Interestingly, she was a professional pitcher on a fast-pitch softball team in the late 1930s before she met my father. Not a hardball pitcher like the women in *A League of Their Own*, the 1992 comedy starring Madonna, Geena Davis, and Tom Hanks; she was an underhand pitcher. She would play four or five games a week and make ten dollars total, about two dollars a game. At one point, she was offered to play on a travel team on which the players made twenty-five dollars a week—pretty good money back in that day. But by then, she had met my father, and he demanded that she stop playing because he wanted her to be home with the kids. I also think that he was jealous of her being seen as successful.

Dad married Mom when she was a teenager, and she was thrust into motherhood, raising two boys from my father's previous marriage. Mom was a hardworking person, just like Dad. She did shift work—from eight in the morning to four in the evening one week, and then midnight to eight in the morning the next week—at a company called Mobile Chemical, a Styrofoam company that manufactured things like meat trays and egg cartons.

I'd like to think that my parents didn't want to be away from their children that much; that's just what it took for them to take care of their family. That's what it took for them to raise six children: me, my two half-brothers, Floyd and Raymond (my dad's first wife died when Raymond was born), and my three biological siblings: Darrell, Roger, and Judy. I was the baby, the youngest. Though my parents' presence was inconsistent in my childhood—which is why my childhood lacked structure—their admirable work ethic stayed with me as I grew older.

Despite Mom's chaotic work schedule, she was around the house more than Dad. She seemed to serve both parenting roles in our household: the mother *and* the father. This always caused some tension for me, I think. But that wasn't her fault. There just seemed to be an indescribable void in my life from not having a father present.

Mom did all that she could, though. I remember her taking time to throw the baseball with me in our yard and her waking up at four thirty in the morning to help me roll newspapers for my paper route. She was the supportive backbone of encouragement in our family. She was the glue.

Mom made you feel like you could do anything in life.

And I was just crazy enough to believe her.

I have written positively about my parents thus far, but the reality is that my childhood was anything but tranquil.

Our yellow stucco, 1,300-square-foot, three-bedroom house sat across the street from the service railroad tracks for the nearby oil refinery, and when the train went by blaring its horn, the walls of our house shook as if there were an earthquake. I guess you could say that this was a picture of my whole childhood: shaky, loud, and chaotic.

Yelling was commonplace in our home. Now that I think about it, anger seemed to be my family's most natural form of expression.

Sometimes things turned violent.

Occasionally, Mom and Dad would have an outburst of angry arguments that would involve physical fights, especially when Dad had been drinking. Sometimes my older brothers would get involved, too—usually to protect Mom. She was the only example of unconditional love that we had, and it was scary to see her treated so horribly.

Once, when I was in fourth grade, I remember waking up and seeing my father's shadow lurking on the wall of my bedroom, which I shared with my brother Roger. There had been a fight a few hours before, and Roger, who was a sophomore in high school at the time, had stood up for Mom. Dad had gone out drinking after the fight.

I remember seeing Dad's five-foot-eight frame hovering over the bed that I shared with Roger, peering at us like a ghost. That's when I saw Dad wind up, shift his body, and—*BAM*—hit Roger as hard as he could right in the jaw.

A brawl broke out.

How Roger wasn't knocked out after that initial blow, I have no idea. All I remember is cowering in the corner, terrified, waiting for the fisticuffs to end.

Thank goodness my parents worked so much, or else our home probably would have been even more violent. Their absence, however, gave us a reprieve.

I didn't learn much about love from Dad but learned everything about love from Mom. It was a rocky and confusing upbringing, but one positive effect the conflict had was that it created a bond of love and commitment between my siblings and me, a connection that still exists today. We all talk to one another multiple times a week, even if it is just for a few minutes.

As a little boy, I thought my parents' anger was their way of taking control of a situation. I'm no psychologist, but I think that what was really happening was that my parents' anger and discontent was hiding something much, much deeper in them: shame and insecurity.

It took a while for me to realize that my home life was not exactly "normal." I remember seeing some of my friends' fathers interacting differently with my buddies—they seemed gentler, loving, and caring. I was sometimes envious when I would see my friends' dads coaching Little League baseball or consoling their children at our games.

Gosh, I *hated* the discourse in our household. But I sort of became numb towards it. It was so common that it almost seemed normal.

The happenings in our household were not apparent to many people on the outside. We did a good job of hiding things, because none of us wanted to admit the dysfunction. Though we were just naturally hiding what any kid would hide, "hiding" what was inside would become a theme in my life.

I'm speculating here—as my parents have since passed away—but I think my father felt a deep sense of shame and insecurity in being uneducated and often felt inadequate and like he was "not good enough," three important words that are a theme of this book. It seems to me that his inability to sift through his shame prevented him from ever moving on or moving forward. Most, if not all, of the toxicity in our household stemmed from my father. His anger ripped through our household like a hurricane, as my mom was left battling the stormy winds, trying to hold everything together.

> *"I went through my life either reacting to my inner angst in an unhealthy way or trying to fill the void created by my insecurities with anything I thought might fulfill me."*

I think that if we cannot appropriately evaluate our pain and shame—becoming aware of the effects they are having on our emotional health—it can be nearly impossible to move beyond them. This was true in my own life, at least. I went through my life either reacting to my inner angst in an unhealthy way or trying to fill the void created by my insecurities with anything I thought might fulfill me.

I believe my dad had a deep regret for what "could have been"—*had he purchased those trucking permits; had he been able to read.* He would sometimes act like he was reading the newspaper, but we all knew that he was only looking at the pictures. It wasn't his fault that he never learned how to read. He left school after third grade to work in the fields and help support his family in Arkansas.

The root of our shame and insecurity oftentimes is not even our fault.

As for my mother I think her shame and insecurity might have stemmed from my father's constant anger towards her, and the reality that she sacrificed her professional softball ambitions for my father: self-respect and unfulfilled dreams. She too had a deep sense of not being good enough. Because of the way my father treated her.

To complicate things even more, I'm also told that my dad was a womanizer when I was really young. He was on the road a lot and was absorbed in a reckless trucking culture. I remember my dad never allowing my sister to work in the potato sheds, and I think that's because he knew the horrible things that took place there.

As I grew up, I was a bit ashamed of my family, and the whole scenario created a void and insecurities within me that I had to deal with later in my life. Please don't misunderstand me: I'm not blaming my family. It is each of our responsibilities to process what has happened in our lives so that we do not project our hurts onto others. But I *didn't* process anything until much later in my life.

I WAS UNAWARE that one of the questions at the heart of my insecurities was this: *What can I do to be loved and accepted?*

I wonder if this is a common insecurity for children with absent fathers or if it is more universal. It seems that this desire for acceptance—and the ways we try to fill this desire outside of who we are in God—is a universal journey.

For me, this insecurity created a longing for two things at a young age: approval and affection. I can tell you that I didn't receive either of these from my father.

Though this void in my own life stemmed from my childhood, the truth is that approval and affection are two of the most sought-after intangibles in our society. I have seen people place their identity in the approval they receive from others and place their comfort in the affection they receive from others. I did the same.

It seems that when our happiness is determined by what we do, not who we are—when our identities hinge upon something on the outside, not the inside—we will inevitably feel empty.

> *"It seems that when our happiness is determined by what we do, not who we are—when our identities hinge upon something on the outside, not the inside—we will inevitably feel empty."*

The great spiritual journey, it seems, is to somehow allow our happiness and contentment to come from within—not from anything on the outside. Christians like myself believe this is attainable through the mystery of grace. The apostle Paul writes in 2 Corinthians 12:9: "My grace is sufficient for you, for power is perfected in weakness." The secret to contentment, I'm learning, is realizing that God's love and grace satisfy our deepest needs.

Maybe your childhood was less traumatic than mine. I pray that it was. But maybe it was more traumatic. Maybe something happened to you later in life—something that was beyond your control—and you became a victim of life's circumstances.

I'm sure you know someone or can identify with the idea that a trauma or difficulty in one's life can birth insecurities. It is natural to attempt to mask these insecurities with an emotion or a pursuit of something.

However, it is important to not suppress insecurities in an attempt to cover them. It's vital to become aware of them and where they might have come from so that we can take intentional steps to move *through* our situations. As Psalm 23:4 says, "Even though I walk *through* the valley of the shadow of death, I fear no evil, for You are with me" (italics added). Whatever shadow you might be walking through, I hope that my experiences might be a comfort and aid to you.

The deep insecurities that we carry may or may not be our faults, but there's a good probability that they are causing pain in our relation-ships. And we *are* responsible for taking care of our relationships.

What's scary is that if we don't deal with what is underneath, we can convince ourselves of things that are not even true. We live in false re-alities. But when we venture into the deep and dark places within our-selves, God can do the miraculous by bringing everything—including what we are most afraid of and ashamed to encounter—into the light, turning brokenness into blessing. We are responsible for encountering what is underneath, because we are all responsible for our choices. We are not born losers. We are not born winners. We are born *choosers*. I hope that we can learn to make better choices because of our increased awareness.

I wish I had become aware earlier of the effect that my rocky child-hood had on my psyche. That was not something I realized until much later in life. And instead of becoming aware, I went through life much like my parents did: either hiding my insecurities or unknowingly re-acting to them.

Identifying Insecurities

- What trials have you endured in your life? What insecurities have arisen from those trials? Where do you think those insecurities come from?

- When those insecurities resurface, how have you tried to hide them? How have you reacted to them?

- What do you usually use to mask your insecurity or shame? Is it an emotion? An action? Something on the exterior like a job or a relationship?

- Read Psalm 23. What is it that you need to move through? Name the valley. What is in the valley? As you name what is in the valley, try to move from the circumstance (examples: divorce, rejection, loss) to the personal emotion or response that the circumstance triggered (examples: bitterness, sadness, despair). What does Psalm 23 say about God's presence as we move through the valley?

CHAPTER 2

What Throwing Potatoes
Taught Me About God

In his book *New Seeds of Contemplation*, Christian writer and contemplative Thomas Merton wrote, "Our idea of God tells us more about ourselves than about Him."

We often project ideas onto God because of our past experiences. This was certainly true in my own life. Anger hung in the air of our household; I breathed it in and exhaled it onto others. And as I grew older, I eventually also exhaled it onto my idea of God.

All of this obviously began in my youth, when anger became a big part of how I reacted to the unsteadiness within me. For example, once in fifth grade, I remember finding out that my sister Judy was going to go sledding in the mountains with her boyfriend. I was upset that she didn't invite me, so when she went outside to get something, I locked her out of the house so she couldn't get back in to gather her belongings for the mountains. Our parents weren't home, so there was nothing they could do to resolve the issue. And there was nothing Judy could do but hysterically pound on the door and beg for me to let her in. For a long time—hours. Seriously.

I just wanted to be included.

It is kind of a funny story, but it is also a reflection of what I did when I was upset or didn't get my way: *I lashed out with anger*. It helped me to think and feel that I was in control. The model that I saw my parents practice became a way of life for me. This became a slippery slope in my life and began a very unhealthy cycle.

Another time I remember hanging out with an older kid from across the street, and we decided to hide behind the bed wall of one of my dad's trucks that had some leftover potatoes inside from the produce he was shipping. We began throwing the potatoes at cars that went past. Sometimes we would hit a vehicle, and it'd make a funny *POW* sound. One time we heard a *screech* as a driver slammed on his breaks and began searching for us. We just assumed that drivers would have no idea where the potatoes were coming from. How dumb were we to legitimately believe that people would think potatoes were falling out of the sky and not coming from the fortress of trucks…my dad's trucks…which were parked right by my parents' home.

> *"The choices you make today—good or bad—will impact your life tomorrow."*

Later that afternoon, after fleeing the scene and returning to my house, I heard a knock on the front door. My dad, who happened to be home at the time, answered the door.

It was a sheriff's deputy from the Kern County Sheriff Department.

"Good afternoon, sir. I'm here because we think it's possible that somebody from your house threw some potatoes at passing cars out of your truck," the sheriff said.

"The windows were down in one of the cars," the sheriff's deputy continued, "and one potato came an inch away from hitting a baby in the head."

The choices you make today—good or bad—will impact your life tomorrow.

My father figured out that it was me. Surprise, surprise. I remember him angrily telling me to "go cut a switch" for him to whip me with—a ritual in our household.

Whenever Dad whipped me with the switch that I cut, there was no formula to the discipline. Sometimes he would make me cut a bigger one that would hurt more. Sometimes he would hit me once. Sometimes he would hit me several times, as if he was taking his own anger out on me. And it *always* hurt.

My usual attire in the summertime was cutoff shorts, no shoes, and no shirt. When he would hit me, I remember the switch sometimes digging into my calves like a whip. I'd have huge welts all over my legs.

Looking back, I think it would have been a good idea for someone to have explained to me what was right and wrong and *why* things were right or wrong instead of just experiencing my father's wrath. There was no molding experience.

I always took my spankings. And when it was over, it was over.

I WAS UNAWARE of how my view of my earthly father would affect how I viewed God when I grew older. The physical punishments I received and the anger my dad portrayed became something that I projected onto God later in my life.

Unknowingly, I formed an unhealthy view of God. And that view of God affected *everything*. Unfortunately, because of my lack of awareness of this, I also feel like I gave my daughters a very unhealthy picture of God through my own parenting style.

When one's spirituality first begins to develop, it is important to ask: Where does my view of God come from?

Thankfully, I had several father-like figures in my life when I ventured through middle school and high school. One of those men was my high school biology teacher, Mr. Newbrough, who invested in me outside of school and who often took me fishing with him on Saturday afternoons. And more than anyone else, my primary father figures during those years were my older biological brothers, Darrell and Roger. They demonstrated the idea of presence to me, something that my father never did, and they even went to father-and-son events with me.

Although my sister, Judy, the matriarch of our family, was not a father figure per se, she was certainly one of my biggest supporters. She still is today. And of course, I always had my mom in the background; she believed in me and made me feel like I could do anything. Looking back I can see that, despite my tumultuous upbringing, God was definitely looking out for me—surrounding me with His love through His people.

> "I projected my experiences with my earthly father upon the God of the Universe. That meant I saw Him as angry, vengeful, distant, impersonal, scary, and—did I mention angry?"

All of this was invaluable for me, but little did I know that the void my father left was always there. This became especially evident in my spirituality, which I began to explore when I was a senior in high school and which I will explain later. But the reason I am telling you about this now is because when I *did* start exploring the idea of a Heavenly Father, I projected my experiences with my earthly father upon the God of the Universe. That meant I saw Him as angry, vengeful, distant, impersonal, scary, and—did I mention angry?

Basically, the God I claimed to believe in was the exact opposite of the loving, forgiving, gracious father that He is—the God we read about in the Bible, who is revealed in the person of Jesus Christ. In my mind, He was someone who, whenever I did something wrong, was going to be mad and angry with me. He was hardly around, but when He did show up, He was there to let me know how displeased He was with my deplorable actions.

This was my early spiritual foundation: *A God who was angry when I did something wrong.*

I will explore this more later on, but it's important to mention it now, because childhood experiences inevitably affect our spirituality and perceptions of God. As author and theologian A.W. Tozer writes in *Knowledge of the Holy*, "What comes into our minds when we think about God is the most important thing about us."

Naming Projections

- Do you believe in God? If so, what do you believe some of God's traits might be?

- What traits might you be projecting onto God because of your own personal experiences? (Consider your perceptions of parents, and think about difficult things you've experienced and teachings you've received.) Are your projections accurate or inaccurate?

- Our understanding of God grows and evolves. How has your perception of God changed over the years?

- What do you think God's reaction is when you mess up? Read 1 John 4:7–21. What does this passage say about God's love and forgiveness?

CHAPTER 3
Fig Leaves and Icebergs

When a person has deep insecurities, the most natural thing is to hide them. As I've mentioned, for me, my anger masked my insecurities. When I got to high school, two additional components emerged that proved to be "masking devices" in my life: playing football and being in romantic relationships.

Though these were my outlets, I challenge you to ponder what yours might be. What techniques have you adopted in your life in an attempt to hide your weaknesses or compensate for them?

Because football is such a large part of my story and because so much happened within me during my formative years, the next several chapters will unfold slowly. It's necessary for me to explain all that was at play within me when I entered adulthood. I've learned that my upbringing and my development were essential in understanding myself. Understanding our childhoods is vital in unmasking our insecurities.

Though the undergirding of anger in my childhood negatively affected my relationships and my view of God as I grew older, anger had its benefits when it came to playing football.

Especially for a player like me who was undersized.

My two older brothers—Roger, who was five feet eleven and five years older than me, and Darrell, who was six feet one and ten years older than me—both had the natural physique to be great football players. They both also weighed over 200 pounds. By the time I got to high school, on the other hand, I was five feet eight and weighed 162 pounds…soaking wet.

I wasn't exactly the typical size of a running back who had hopes of playing football in college. But I was determined and motivated. And anger was the fuel of my fire.

Besides, football was a sort of a religion in the Bakersfield area. Playing football had been my dream since I was a child.

When I was younger, I remember climbing the fence with my friends on Friday nights at North High School's football field and sneaking into the games to watch my brothers and local heroes play. We watched the games in awe, as if watching a fireworks show, thinking and dreaming about the day when we too might be able to wear that red and gray North High jersey and play for their legendary coach, Turk Eliades.

If football was a religion in our community, and it certainly was for me and my friends, then the bishops were Turk Eliades and Paul Briggs. Those two men, both World War II veterans, coached against one another for *over three decades*—Coach Eliades at the helm of the North High Stars and Coach Briggs at the helm of the Bakersfield High Drillers.

North High (Eliades) versus Bakersfield (Briggs) was your typical David versus Goliath rivalry. At the time, North High had under a thousand students in its school, and the majority were white—mostly because of the blue-collar Caucasian "Okies" and "Arkies" working in the oil refineries. Bakersfield had thousands of students and a more diverse racial breakdown. At one point, it was the largest high school in Central California. There was also an obvious socioeconomic difference between the people at North High and the people at Bakersfield High. Most referred to those at North High as "River Rats"—and yes, as I mentioned, that was a derogatory term when used by people from Bakersfield. When it came to football, Bakersfield was the top school in that part of the valley, and it had a lot of history—producing players like Pro Football Hall of Famer Frank Gifford, four-time Pro Bowler Jeff Siemon, and five-time Pro Bowler Louis Wright, to name a few.

But seeing Coach Eliades on the sidelines when I was a kid was like looking at a celebrity or an icon. He was someone who stood *with* us. Someone who stood *for* us.

Coach Eliades was a Greek man who grew up in McGill, Nevada, a small town near Ely. He came from an oppressed, dismembered people group—a bunch of Greek miners in the Wild West. As a young man, he was drafted into World War II, and his plane was shot down just outside Berlin, Germany, where he was held as a prisoner of war. He was eventually freed by, no, not the Americans, but the Russians—but that's another story. A series of unlikely circumstances after World

War II landed Coach Eliades in Oildale, where he coached football and taught mathematics at North High for thirty-two years.

Though he had many opportunities to leave Oildale, Coach Eliades had no desire to go elsewhere. Oildale was where he decided to plant his roots and raise his family, and he became a fixture in the community. I'm theorizing here, but I think he remained in Oildale because he knew what it was like to be a part of a people group and community that was looked down upon. I think that he always connected Oildale with his upbringing in Ely. I remember him often saying to us, "The game of football is like going to war, and you want to stay close to those you trust." For him, the people he trusted were his family, his former players, and the humble, down-to-earth people of Oildale.

In December 2016, Coach Eliades died in his Oildale home of forty years. He was ninety-three years old. I'm confident that there is no other place on this planet where he would have preferred to have his last breaths.

Football became a transformative tool for me—especially in my high school years. And, it turns out, I was pretty good at football.

After playing junior varsity my freshman year, I played varsity my next three seasons (though I will only cover my first three years of high school in this chapter). Overall, I rushed for 2,400 yards in my high school career as a running back—becoming one of the top ball carriers in North High's history, which still surprises me today.

I wasn't your typical running back. I was a small, white guy who wasn't the fastest player on the field. When I speak to groups today and am introduced with a string of football accolades attached to my name, I'm often met with curious eyes, wondering if I am a fill-in for who the speaker was supposed to be showing up. I'm sure people Google my name when they get home, curious if I was lying about the whole ordeal. I'm proof that God has a sense of humor.

But that's what made North High a perfect match for me. We were both small. Overlooked. Unassuming. We both had pasts that were often frowned upon, judged, and labeled.

On the football team, for perhaps the first time in my life, I felt a real sense of pride in who I was and what I was doing. I was *part* of something. I *belonged*. My coach *believed in me*. The fans and community showered me with approval and affection—things that I had been searching for. And when I was playing football, I felt a sense of fulfillment that I didn't experience anywhere else.

In addition, Coach Eliades taught those who played for him some profound life lessons. I think it's safe for me to say that what I am about to state is on behalf of a whole lot of guys who played football for Coach Eliades. Through football, we learned what it meant to be selfless and build teamwork and to do it by being humble. Coach's stories about World War II gave us a picture of what it meant to be a part of something that was meaningful and worth fighting for, like the North High football tradition. He taught us about the opportunities that life presents to each one of us: the potential to truly *live*; the potential to *accomplish* something *together*. That's the beauty of football: It takes eleven people on the field working together to make something happen.

My former teammates and I all wish that someone had recorded some of Coach's pregame pep talks. He had a way of inspiring his players to give the most they could every Friday night. I remember being moved to tears multiple times because of one of his speeches before running out onto the field. Though he was shy about sharing stories from the war, Coach Eliades would sometimes talk about his captivity, his freedom, and all the horrible things that he saw the Russians doing to the Germans in Berlin. Then he would somehow bring the lessons he learned from the war to the presence of the game and would remind us that life was unbelievably frail and precious. He always said just enough to give us a glimpse of what it was like to go to war with other soldiers.

"See this little bit of your finger?" he would sometimes say with his loud Greek voice, pointing to a tiny portion of his pinkie finger. "That represents tonight, just a *tiny* bit of your life—but you might talk about this night for the rest of your life! You will regret it if you don't walk off that field knowing that you left everything out there—for this school and for those who went before you."

In my junior season, our team played every game like it was our last. And, just like Coach Eliades always said, it indeed turned out to be a season that we would talk about for the rest of our lives.

The storyline that year was that we, like any classic underdogs, were on a mission to prove people wrong. And we set the tone that we were on a mission right from the start. The year before, several of the players on the team had been caught drinking at a party and had been lightly disciplined, so my junior year, we had a players-only meeting at the start of season and set the precedent and tone for the team: if anyone was found drinking or carousing, they would be reported to the coaches and kicked off the team. Apparently a couple of the players didn't think we were serious, because we found out a few weeks later that they had been drinking. Well, we went to the coaches and reported them, and they were kicked off the team. These were not only our friends—they were also starters. But we were on a mission.

Before we played our first game of the year, however, North High's football program was struck by an incomprehensible tragedy. Our teammate and friend Sonny Anderson was killed in a car accident on his way to the beach at the end of August. (I had gone to the coast with Sonny before, and he had asked me if I wanted to go that particular weekend, but I had other obligations.)

Sonny's death left a gaping hole in our hearts. After Sonny's funeral, it felt like we spent every waking minute at Sonny's mom's house. I remember Coach Eliades gathering all of us together and simply saying, "There is a time and place for everything, and it was his time to go."

If we weren't determined as a team before, we were *really* determined then. Playing in memory of Sonny became our rallying cry throughout the season. We went on a momentous ride…

There were four high schools in our area: Foothill, East, Bakersfield, and North (us). Every single one of them was undefeated my junior year. That is, until we played them.

We beat Foothill, and the newspapers said, "That was good win, but wait until they play East."

We beat East, and the newspapers said, "That was a good win, but wait until they play Bakersfield High."

It didn't matter who we beat; we couldn't get any respect!

And then came our game against Bakersfield High. Another Eliades versus Briggs matchup.

We were undefeated. They were undefeated. They had Theopolis Bell, a highly touted wide receiver who went on to receive a full ride from the University of Arizona and to eventually win two Super Bowls with the Pittsburgh Steelers.

But we won. Again.

And eventually we became the only undefeated team that Coach Eliades ever coached. It was a magical season.

The lessons we learned are what I remember most from that historical year. In the wake of Sonny's passing, Coach Eliades taught us that we did not have to be defined by life's circumstances. And as the season unfolded, Coach taught us that we didn't have to be defined by what the media or community said about us; we weren't defined by their perceptions.

It didn't matter that Bakersfield High was several times bigger than us. It didn't matter that they had an esteemed history and we didn't or that they had won state championships and we hadn't. Coach Eliades told us we could still beat them and prove to everyone that we were for real.

And Coach Eliades could teach it because he lived it.

Though he grew up in a neglected community, Coach Eliades didn't let that define him. Though his father died in a mining accident when he was in college, he didn't let that loss define him. Though he experienced the traumas of World War II, he didn't let those struggles define him. He always pressed on through the pain. No, he did not avoid the pain or suppress it. He pressed on *through* it. He was like the people of Oildale: he worked hard, perhaps because it was the only thing he could do.

Life, Coach Eliades believed, was too much of a *gift to* him for him to become a *victim of* it.

I WAS UNAWARE that my search for approval affection was beginning to negatively influence my identity. Though the positive emotions I associated with football were instrumental for my confidence during those years—a healthy outlet for me to invest myself and grow as a man—I was also beginning to find my identity in football. My identity hinged on what I did rather than who I was. And that's because I didn't know who I was.

But this search for affection and approval didn't stop at football.

Football seemed to temporarily fill the "approval" void, but, to be candid, one way I attempted to fill the "affection" void was through sex. In seventh grade, I had already lost my virginity. By the time I was in high school, I had been with a lot of different girls. I was needy for affection and intimacy. The affection that I got from sex was a level of satisfaction—not just physically, but also emotionally—that I had never felt before. Plus, my family life did not really include closeness, intimacy, or affection. For those who were in my life during that period of time and who were probably hurt by my actions, I feel remorseful, and I'm sorry.

Now I can see that I was merely filling a void. I never drank or smoked or partied like many of peers (my dad did that, and I didn't want to be like him), but being in physically unhealthy relationships was my attempt to fill a deep emotional need. Don't we all seem to go searching for love outside of God—thinking other things will fulfill us?

Just as we read in the Genesis story that Adam and Eve sewed fig leaves together to hide their shame with clothing, I used football and sex to attempt to hide my shame. In Peter Scazzero's book *Emotionally Healthy Spirituality*, he uses the metaphor of an iceberg to describe our emotional lives. What's interesting about an iceberg is that seven-eighths of it is below the waterline, making only a small section of it plainly visible. Just like an iceberg, the reality of our existence is beneath the surface. And so despite my positive experiences on the football field during my first three years of high school, a lot of junk was going on beneath the surface—a lot more than I even realized at the time.

> *"When you excel at something—or when you find other means to receive affection and approval—it can do wonders in hiding what you don't want others to see."*

When you excel at something—or when you find other means to receive affection and approval—it can do wonders in hiding what you don't want others to see.

Masks and Facades

- It's easy to create a false projection of yourself for others to see, especially through the avenue of social media. What do you want others to think of you? What do you want to hide?

- Returning to a metaphor in this chapter, if you are an iceberg, what is beneath the surface? What is above the surface?

- When I was performing as a football player, the success I experienced helped to hide the insecurities that I didn't want others to see. How do you perform for others? What components make up the shell that hides your insecurity or shame?

- What are you more focused on—the development of your exterior shell that you want others to see or the development of your interior life? In which ways are you crafting an image you want others to see? What are you doing to develop your interior life?

- Read Genesis 3 and consider the natural human tendency to hide our shame, our nakedness. What's your fig leaf, your covering?

CHAPTER 4
Too Small, Too Slow

The next phase of my life was decided by an unlikely person: the head coach of our archrival, Paul Briggs of Bakersfield High. Not to belabor my high school experience, but Coach Briggs' role in my life during this time would have an enormous impact on my spirit and psyche moving forward.

To begin, the football team my senior year wasn't as good as our undefeated team from junior year. My senior year, our team ended up finishing in a three-way tie for first place in our conference, the South Yosemite League. But because of a silly conference rule at the time, the defending conference champions (us) were automatically disqualified if there was a tie for first-place. Still, we had been part of a special era of North High football that included the best season in the school's history—as well as Coach Eliades' only undefeated season in his coaching career.

Coach Eliades was an old-school gentleman when it came to his players going on to play collegiate football beyond North High. He held the belief that if his North High players were good enough to play football at the next level, then they ought to play a couple of years at the local junior college—Bakersfield College (BC)—before going to a bigger university of their choice. Because North High was so small, playing at a junior college made for a more natural, stair-step transition to the next level. Also, Coach Eliades was best friends with the head coach at BC. Coach was a loyal person—a military man, someone who had risen above all odds as a Greek growing up in Ely—and I think he tried to push his players to BC because of his sense of loyalty.

Thing is, to put it bluntly, I didn't want to play for the head coach at BC.

As much of a role model as Coach Eliades was for me (and continued to be to me throughout the remainder of his long life), my unwillingness to attend BC did cause some friction between us my senior year. He wanted me to play at Bakersfield College, and I, frankly, didn't want to play there.

One day during the second semester of my senior season, I received a call from Coach Briggs. This wasn't as strange as it might seem. Having grown up in the area, he had seen me go through the ranks of Pop Warner football, and we always had a great relationship and friendship. Years later, he would sometimes say to me, "Man, I wish you could've played at Bakersfield High; it's not fair that you went to North High." That was a nice thing for him to say considering the players he had coached.

Our conversation that day, however, *was* strange. "Randy, I don't know how to tell you this," he said, "but I've sent several college recruiting coaches over to North High, and Coach Eliades is discouraging them and saying that you aren't big enough or fast enough, that you need a couple of years in junior college."

"What?" I questioned, shocked. "I had no idea that I was even being recruited."

"Yeah," he affirmed. "This is what I'm going to do. I'm going to give them your phone number, and I will show them all the films on you that they need to see."

"Wow, thanks, Coach," I said.

I knew how big of a deal this was, because whenever recruiters came to town, there were two coaches they talked to: Coach Briggs and Coach Eliades. If Coach Eliades wasn't telling recruiters about me, then I was in trouble. That is, unless Coach Briggs told them about me. I had found it puzzling that some of the schools that had started to recruit me early on had turned cold. After receiving that call from Coach Briggs, however, it all made sense.

Whereas Coach Eliades had been one of my biggest supporters at North High, Coach Briggs became my biggest supporter in helping me find a college that was right for me at the next level. Turns out, Coach Briggs had done that same thing for many competing high school players—including my best friend Bill Nichols, a fellow halfback, the year before.

It wasn't that Coach Eliades didn't believe that I could play at the next level. For example, my senior year, there was a local newspaper article titled "Rich Not Big or Fast, He Just Wins," where Coach Eliades was quoted saying: "Wherever he goes on to play…he will do them a good job and then people will realize what this game basically comes down to is a person's heart. You don't have to be big or fast…"

See, I think Coach Eliades just wanted me to play at BC *first*.

Before he passed away, I sometimes gave Coach Eliades a hard time and told him, "You didn't want me to play at a big school because you thought I was too small and too slow!"

"Ahhhh, Rrrandeeey, I don't want to talk about that," he would say.

We could laugh about it. And that's the truth. I never held that against Coach Eliades. I loved him until the day he died. I'll forever be indebted to him because of the values that he instilled in me.

Having Coach Briggs on my side, however, was pivotal for me. Recruiters had a lot of doubts about my abilities. The two things that I did not have—speed and size—were the two things that most recruiters looked for. They figured they could teach skills to a player. But the running back *had* to have those two things.

But the full-fledged support of not only one of the most respected coaches in the state of California but also an *opposing* coach seemed to give recruiters the confidence to pursue me. Had it not been for Coach Briggs, who knows where I would have ended up.

Overall, Coach Briggs's support of me during this phase of my life helped to water some of the seeds that Coach Eliades, Mr. Newbrough, my siblings, and my mom had already planted. Again, there was someone who believed in me. Someone who was willing to put himself out there for me. Looking back, it's absolutely mind-blowing to me that God placed the people in my life that He did at each step of my journey.

Many labels had been placed on me by pundits in the community who doubted my abilities: "He's too small for the next level." "He's too slow for the next level." "He's a good high school halfback, and he'll do okay at a junior college, but he won't stand a chance at a big NCAA school." "He'll never be anything more than a good high school running back."

Coach Briggs reminded me that if he believed in me, then I could believe in myself. If he saw greatness in me, then I could see greatness in myself.

If you don't have a strong foundation or understanding of who you are and what you can be, it's easy to believe what others say about you. Actually, it's easy to believe what others say about you no matter what your upbringing is, because words and labels can be powerful, especially during formative years.

> "If you don't have a strong foundation or understanding of who you are and what you can be, it's easy to believe what others say about you."

Coach Briggs metaphorically removed all those labels just by believing in me. He showed me that I am more than the labels that others put on me.

Sure, I might've been small. Sure, I might've been a little slower than most running backs. But that didn't mean I couldn't go on to play at a big Division I university. And it didn't mean that I couldn't dream of playing in the NFL.

I WAS BEGINNING TO UNDERSTAND early on in my life that people will try to label you, categorize you, and put limits on you and your abilities. But thanks to Coach Briggs, I learned that what people said about me did not define me. And, just as Coach Eliades said in the newspaper quote, you can never judge a player's heart. I relate this to 1 Samuel 16:7: "Do not look at his appearance or at the height of his stature, because I have rejected him; for God sees not as man sees, for man looks at the outward appearance, but the Lord looks at the heart." I recognize that in this passage, the Lord is speaking about the character and heart for service, but I believe that statement carries weight when considering anything for your life.

At some point, all of us in some way feel small because of our insecurities or struggles. Some of us don't feel adequate. Most of us, in some way, do not feel like we are enough. But 2 Corinthians 3:4–6 says that our adequacy is in Christ Jesus.

God has put a dream in each one of us. He has a plan and a purpose for each one of us—to do something that is unique and special. Though we might sometimes doubt if we can really pursue our dreams, all things are possible with God. He put a dream inside each of us, and He strengthens us on our journeys.

I love the story in 1 Samuel 16 in which Samuel, a Hebrew prophet, visits David's family in search for a new king but isn't content in selecting any of David's siblings. Samuel asks David's father, "Don't you have any other sons?" The father points him to the young, small, frail, emotional, unassuming boy out in the field shepherding the sheep. This boy, David, was the one who ultimately defeated the giant Goliath and became king.

Just like God picked David, He handpicked you to do something special, too. God can defeat your giants *in* you and *through* you if you trust Him.

When I speak to students today, one of my main objectives is to empower them to remove the false labels they've accepted. We need to understand that labels are nothing but fables—lies that affect our self-worth and our identity. We must consciously identify them as lies and then remove them.

> *"God has put a dream in each one of us. He has a plan and a purpose for each one of us—to do something that is unique and special. Though we might sometimes doubt if we can really pursue our dreams, all things are possible with God. He put a dream inside each of us, and He strengthens us on our journeys."*

This is what Coach Briggs did for me: he empowered me to remove the labels that others had put on me—even labels that my own coach put on me to steer me to junior college. My ability to remove those labels is what mentally prepared me for the next phase of my football career. Similarly, your ability to remove the labels that you or others have put on you will prepare you for the next thing that God has planned for you.

The other day, a friend approached me and said, "Randy, my son *really* wants to play football, but he's so small and lanky. I know that you played, but you were one in a million. Would you mind giving him a call and explaining to him that he's too small and skinny to play a sport like football? I think he'll listen if it comes from you."

"What? Tell him that he has no chance? I'm sorry. I can't do that," I told my friend. "Don't ever tell him he can't do something. Whatever he has in his heart to do, you have to stand behind him and support him and encourage him."

I never want anyone to believe that they can't do something that they are passionate about simply because an outside source says that they can't. That's just noise. Had I listened to the noise, I might have abandoned my dream of playing football at the next level. Had I abandoned that dream, I might have looked back on my life with regret, wondering what could have been.

Just because you shed a label doesn't mean you will be able to achieve you dream. But you'll be better positioned to achieve it. And I believe that everyone should feel like they can pursue their dreams. Plus, isn't it better to have a big dream that you don't achieve than a small dream that you do achieve?

When we pursue our dreams, even if we fail, we can reflect on our pursuits without regret, knowing that we gave our all. And we can learn incredible truths about ourselves in pursuit of that which makes us feel most alive.

One time after I spoke at a grade school, a precious young boy gave me a card with the names and numbers of his parents and a note that said, "Please call them. They don't believe that I can do anything." Can you believe how that young person must've felt? How hurt he must've been and how much trust he had to share that?

My heart sank when I read that note. It would have been inappropriate for me to call his parents and tell them how to raise their child, but I still pray for that boy, hoping that he will continue to remove the labels that others have put on him, hoping that he will believe in himself and feel valued for who he is.

Labels have never been more damaging than they are today. Social media allows cowards and haters to hide behind a computer keyboard while belittling someone else. I hear stories all the time about someone who committed suicide because of something that was said about him or her on social media. If we recognized the effect that labels have on others, then perhaps we would never dare to categorize people or tear them down.

By now I am convinced that removing our labels is a lifelong process. And though Coach Briggs helped me to remove the labels that others had placed on me regarding my football performance, another set of labels formed as I ventured through life. And these labels went much deeper than football. They were labels on my soul, on the depths of who I am. They were labels that I put on myself.

Labels and Noise

- What are some of the labels that others have put on you? Name them. Become aware of them.

- Do you believe the labels? Why or why not?

- What would it take for you to remove the labels—now and moving forward? (Removing the labels is not a one-time thing. It involves conditioning your mind to never believe them again, and when the labels *do* resurface, you have to recognize that they have returned.)

- What mental checks could you put in place today to keep yourself from believing the lies people speak about you?

- Read 1 Samuel 16:1–13, a story about the unexpected anointing of a David, a young shepherd boy whose father believed he could not be a king. What labels did David's own family put on him? Meditate on 1 Samuel 16:7, and compare God's standards to the human standards listed in the passage.

CHAPTER 5
From Hawaii to Hell

I had four best friends in high school: Bill, Mark, Rick, and Skip. A few of us started a band together back then that was called Mothers' Mess (we were indeed our mothers' mess!). I played rhythm guitar and sang. Thank goodness we didn't have the technology back then that we have now; I'm glad none of those recordings live on through our iTunes libraries and that none of our shows can be seen on YouTube. But we were hot stuff then. Well, we like to think that we were, at least.

Bill, Mark, Rick, and Skip were all one year ahead of me. For whatever reason, I mostly hung out with people who were older. I just didn't relate to what those in my class were experiencing.

All that to say, while they were off at college and moving into the next phases of their lives, I was finishing my senior year at North High. We all remained best friends and hung out whenever we could. I might have had less of a social life my senior year, but I was focused on my future anyway.

At Christmas break my senior year, I remember Mark returning home and hanging out with me. As we spent time together, I remember listening to him tell me about someone he had met at college—someone who he said had changed his life. I thought that he was talking about a girl, which is why I was dumbfounded when he said that the someone was Jesus Christ.

What did he mean? How could he talk about someone imaginary as if he were a real person he could have a personal relationship with?

I had some friends who went to church, but it all seemed silly and difficult to understand. Though religion made little sense to me, I was truly happy for Mark. There was an excitement in his voice that made me as happy for him about his newfound faith as I would have been about any other positive experience in his life.

"I believe that God has a plan for my life," Mark told me. "I've never felt happier. Have you ever thought about having a relationship with

Christ?"

"Mark, it sounds really good, but I'm gonna have to think about it for a while," I told him.

Mark didn't bring it up again. We continued hanging out as we normally did. He had no agenda. He was my friend and was simply sharing with me what was happening in his life.

But the conversation that we had impacted me moving forward.

The next semester, in the spring, I was recruited by a number of big Division I schools, thanks to Coach Briggs. In my recruiting questionnaires, I'd said that I was interested in fishing, hunting, and Christianity—yes, Christianity! All because of Mark. He had piqued my interest, and I'd decided that I wanted to further explore the idea.

It might seem odd for me, a non-Christian at the time who didn't know a thing about God, to be so bold as to write Christianity on my recruiting questionnaires, but it just seemed like the right thing to do. If Jesus Christ could impact my best friend so deeply, then I figured I ought to at least learn more about what Mark was talking about. College seemed like a good time to dive into some of the questions that I had about life.

By March, I had narrowed my college selection down to Arizona State University, coached by Frank Kush, one of the most ruthless college coaches ever, and the University of New Mexico (UNM), coached by Rudy Feldman.

All it took, oddly, was a visit to Arizona State for me to decide that I wanted to play at UNM. There were probably twenty other recruits at Arizona State, and we were treated like slabs of meat going through a processing plant. I don't even think they looked at my recruiting questionnaire. I felt like another number, another body.

I visited UNM the next week, which is where my brother Darrell had gone on a track scholarship, and my experience was the opposite of that at Arizona State. It was personal, and I felt wanted and pursued. The defensive backs coach took me fishing one afternoon, and another coach introduced me to two men named Dan and Jay, who worked for Campus Crusade for Christ. I could tell that the kind people at UNM had read my recruiting questionnaire and really wanted me to attend their university.

I committed and signed with the Lobos.

Once again, I was overcome with gratitude for Coach Briggs and everything he'd done to get my name in front of recruiters. I wanted to play football at an NCAA Division I school, not the local junior college, and I had Coach Briggs to thank for making that a reality.

Not only did Coach Briggs work tirelessly to get my game film in front of recruiters, but he, along with my brother Darrell who coached at Paso Robles High School, also submitted my name for a high school all-star game in Hawaii the summer heading into my freshman year at UNM. The game was between California's high school all-stars and Hawaii's high school all-stars. "I know the coach down there," Coach Briggs told me, "and I'm going to tell them that you need to be on the team."

I ended up being selected—one of only twenty-eight guys from the entire state of California.

The conversation that Mark and I had over Christmas break probably helped lead to my agreement to attend a Fellowship of Christian Athletes (FCA) football camp in Santa Barbara, California, the summer after my senior year, a couple months before the high school all-star game in Hawaii. A generous man in Bakersfield offered to pay my way, and I decided to attend because, one, it was free, and, two, I was promised that I would get to meet professional football players. I didn't know anyone who was going. But I decided to go anyway.

At the FCA camp, I remember meeting people like Paul Anderson, heralded the strongest man in the world at the time (not a football player, but interesting nonetheless); Minnesota Vikings kicker Fred Cox, who to this day is the organization's all-time leading scorer; and Cleveland Browns punter-kicker Don Cockroft.

The final evening, Don Cockroft shared his faith testimony, and out of the 1,200 guys there in attendance, I felt like he was speaking to me. I remember Don saying, "When you accomplish everything you set out to do and you still feel empty, it's because that emptiness is a void that can only be filled by God."

This resonated with me because I had just finished high school and had accomplished several goals that were big for me—goals that I thought would make me happy. But there was still a void. In my dorm room that night, I prayed, "If you want me, God, here I am," and I asked Christ to come into my life.

It was as if I knew that I needed something, and if it was God that I needed, then I confirmed it that night. For the first time, some of the things that Mark had told me months before began to make some sense. But it took some time for me to fully grasp what I had confessed. I had no idea of the impact that attending that FCA camp had on my life until several years later.

Let's be clear about something: my insecurities didn't dissolve the moment I accepted Christ. There was a lot going on within me. All I knew was that it seemed as if I had a new hope for my life.

I was a Christian. And I had Don Cockroft and my best friend Mark to thank.

Later that summer, I began preparing for the high school all-star game—a fifteen-day, all-expense-paid trip to Hawaii, all thanks to Coach Briggs and my brother Darrell. Turns out, my experience in Hawaii had a massive impact on my life.

I was very excited to be in the game. Much like during the recruiting process, I felt like my world was opening up. There I was, flying across the ocean on a 747 and then checking into a five-star hotel. I was only a kid, a boy from Oildale, California.

When practice began, I found out that the coaches were playing me as a cornerback instead of a running back, so I asked them for an opportunity to fight for the starting running back spot. I excelled at mini-camp and became the starting running back—in front of a back who had a full ride to the University of Washington and another who went on to play in the NFL after college. I was very pleased and motivated.

The day before our big game between the Californians and the Hawaiians, however, I received a haunting phone call from back home. I got the news that Mark, one of my best friends and the person who had told me about Jesus months before, had been killed by a drunk driver. Four kids my age were in the car, and only two had survived. Danny Eliades, Coach Eliades's son, had been in the car and had suffered major head injuries. He was never the same after that accident.

Mark had inspired me to write "Christianity" down on my recruiting questionnaires, and he had influenced me to attend the FCA camp where I had accepted Christ. I was very confused about what God was doing after hearing about Mark's death. I was shocked, stunned, and distraught.

Sadly, this had become a theme within the football program at North High.

First, Sonny Anderson had passed away. Then, just a couple months before my trip to Hawaii, my good friend and North High teammate Ronnie Boleschka had died in a car accident. Then Mark's life was snuffed out, which caused a lot of questions in our community.

What was going on? Was this just how life was, with young people dying all the time?

Honestly, I thought that I might die next. It was bizarre how many of my close friends had been killed. Sonny, Ronnie, and Mark. All gone within a two-year span.

In Hawaii, I bluntly prayed, "What kind of plan is this, God? What kind of plan is this that you would take Mark's life?"

> "In Hawaii, I bluntly prayed, 'What kind of plan is this, God? What kind of plan is this that you would take Mark's life?'"

That night at the game, I played with a vengeance. I played in memory of Mark but with a vengeance against reality—against God, perhaps. I was angry about life and about the fact that so many of my friends' lives had been taken.

To this day, I don't remember much of the game. I was in a different world. Turns out, I rushed for seventy yards, scored a touchdown, and helped our team of Californians win 21–0. I took out all my anger on those poor Hawaiians.

I flew home the next day and went to Mark's funeral that next week. I was a pall-bearer.

Though I was supposed to move into a dorm at UNM for the start of training camp, I called my coaches and told them what was going on. I needed to be in Oildale.

I remember feeling terrified and uneasy the day of the funeral. Seeing Mark's casket made me sick to my stomach. Talking to our friends and his relatives that day made my heart ache. Seeing all my teammates at a funeral home—again—was sobering and haunting.

It didn't seem right that we should have to go through this: the horror of watching a mother lose her son, the torment of watching friends lose friends.

And as I neared my freshman year at UNM, I felt more insecure and angry and lost than ever before.

I WAS UNAWARE that loss and life's unexpected circumstances can add layers of complexity to insecurities that already exist. There was a lot building up within me, and I had no idea how to deal with it. And heading into college, I had the mindset that I was going to do exactly what I had done in Hawaii: harness my anger and aggression and unleash it on the football field.

My frantic mental and emotional state as I entered college was reminiscent of something that happened to my sister and me in elementary school while we were riding our aunt's horse, Tiny....

Once on a hot summer day, my sister Judy and I rode Tiny down to the Kern River for a swim, one of our favorite things to do. As we were making our way down the bank toward the river—me in the front, Judy in the back—Tiny collapsed, catapulting us into the river. When I came up out of the water and regained my composure, I saw Tiny's body convulsing in the water. Terrified, Judy and I grabbed Tiny's neck and head to stabilize her.

I had no idea that she was dying. All I knew was that I needed to find help, so I took off sprinting toward the town. I ran barefoot for over a mile on that 110-degree summer day. The hot sand burned the soles of my feet, but I didn't care; I was panicking. I cried all the way—completely shocked and distraught. I eventually knocked on the door of the first house I came to and asked the person if I could call my mom, but Tiny had already died. The veterinarian believed that she had a brain clot from when she had bashed her head on a train trestle months before.

I share this story because I was in a similar state of shock heading into my freshman year at college. I was proverbially running from the trauma of Mark's death, crying and distraught. I had no idea what to make of it all. No idea how to process what was unfolding in my life. No idea why all the death was happening.

I do not think that I ever adequately processed the various losses from my childhood through high school—the loss of my horse; the loss of my aunts, uncles, and grandparents; and the loss of my close friends. If you have experienced any element of loss (and most have), it's imperative—vitally important—that you find somebody to trust in your life. A mentor. A therapist. A spiritual leader. Someone who you can talk to and confide in. It's important that you find people who have gone before you, lived longer, and experienced life deeper to help navigate you through your emotions and thoughts regarding traumatic experiences. The more you hide your difficult experiences by not talking about them, the cloudier and uglier they can become over time.

For me, football became even more of a coping mechanism. It was a way to bury myself in something that I was good at and a way to seem meaningful to an awful lot of people. Not only had my performance in football become a fig leaf to cover my insecurities; it had also become a sort of ledge for me to cling to when I was falling. Although football wasn't bad in and of itself, I wish I would have channeled my hurt and frustration through a more appropriate outlet—God. But instead my insecurities plunged deeper, and I elevated football (and my performance in football) even higher.

Loss and Trauma

- What loss have you experienced in your own life? The death of a loved one or a friend? The loss of a job or a dream? The loss of a relationship or friendship?

- How have you dealt with this loss? What was your reaction to the loss? What preexisting insecurities did the loss enhance?

- What are some of the things today that trigger past hurts you have not dealt with?

- What do you cling to when your insecurities resurface? What do you elevate? Is it a performance of some sort?

- Read Jesus's response to the Pharisees in Matthew 23. How did the Pharisees' obsession with their performance prevent them from healthy emotional living—with themselves and with others?

CHAPTER 6
Capitalistic Christianity

To speed things up after diving deep into my formative high school years, I will write briefly about my college experience and football career at the University of New Mexico; I'll cover my college football career in this chapter.

What I feel is most important to know about these years is that, though I entered college with fears and insecurities, both my football career and spiritual growth were on the up-and-up during my time as a student athlete in Albuquerque. I parallel them with one another throughout this chapter—going back and forth between football and my personal life—to demonstrate the positives I experienced both on and off the field.

Spiritually, although a lot of students go to college and lose their faith, my experience was the opposite: college is where I began to grow in my faith. But it's important to note that even as this positive and beneficial exploration of faith was taking place, I was also beginning to project my own life experiences and insecurities onto my relationship with God.

Overall, though there were a few setbacks (and though there was a lot that was still taking place beneath the surface), those first three and a half semesters at UNM were generally positive. It wasn't until my final semester, which I will cover next chapter, that my shame and insecurities were exposed.

At the beginning of training camp my freshman year, head coach Rudy Feldman called me into his office and asked me, "Do you want to play running back on the freshmen team this year, or would you like to have a chance to play defensive back on the varsity squad?" My freshman year with the Lobos happened to be the same year that the NCAA passed a new ruling that allowed freshmen to play on the varsity squad.

I thought about it for a few seconds and then said, "Coach, I'd like to play varsity."

Though the running back position was one that I really enjoyed and one that had brought me a lot of success in high school, I wanted to play varsity. Plus, I had caught a glimpse of what college football might be like during training camp and figured that it was better for me, with my lack of size at this level, to be one of eleven guys on defense chasing after an opposing player rather than having eleven defenders—big, strong defenders—chasing after me as a running back. Simple logic.

My decision to play defensive back ended up being one of the best decisions I ever made. To have any chance of playing college football at the Division I level, my best possibility was as a defensive back.

My defensive backs coach during my first year at UNM, John Becker, helped me learn the nuances of the position, and, as it turns out, I really enjoyed the defensive backfield. I loved the complexities and the strategies involved in playing defense.

I ended up starting the second game of the season against the University of Houston, becoming the first freshman to start in a defensive position in the history of UNM. I even had an interception during my first game—a pass that was thrown deep down the sideline that I intercepted in the corner of the end zone.

My career at UNM had a good start.

It felt like UNM was a perfect fit for me off the football field my freshman year, too. One reason is because I was growing in my faith like never before.

Two men, Dan and Jay, of Campus Crusade for Christ (known today as Cru), became my primary spiritual mentors. Dan later became a pastor at Grace Community Church in Albuquerque, and, though Jay went through a divorce my sophomore year and left his ministry post, his influence resurfaced later in my life.

My freshman year, I found myself learning simple truths about what it meant to be a Christian. The way I looked at reality started to change.

That year I remember wishing that my high school buddy Mark was still alive. I wanted to thank him for the seeds that he had planted in my life months before. The more I began to understand about eternal life and God's plan, the more I began to believe that I would one day see him again.

By my sophomore year, I was also returning punts and kicks for the Lobos. I became one of the top-ranked returners in the country and flourished in that position on special teams by my senior year.

Defensively, I led the team with three fumble recoveries and 111 tackles as a sophomore, which earned me the Colonel H.J. Golightly Defensive MVP team award. I also received All-WAC honors my sophomore year.

Please understand that by sharing with you some of these stats and accolades, I am by no means bragging. I only want to demonstrate that I found my niche as a defensive back and was having success.

I also got a new defensive backs coach my sophomore year: Andy Christoff, the best position coach I had in college. Coach Christoff was savvy and was instrumental in my development as a player. His outgoing personality reminded me of singer and funny man Dean Martin. Coach Christoff used to chew tobacco like it was going out of style. He always had a big ol' lump in his jaw. One day during our defensive backs meeting right before he game, he was explaining the game plan to us in the locker room when he suddenly began looking around, needing to spit. There was no trashcan nearby, so he simply opened up his coat pocket and spit into it. My fellow defensive backs and I still laugh about that today.

Most importantly, Coach Christoff understood the secrets of playing in the secondary. The reads. The footwork. The value and importance of positioning. He took me under his wing and turned me into a top-level defensive back. I worked hard—really hard—trying to apply all the things that he taught us.

When I signed and committed to the Lobos, I had no idea what to expect. But two years later, I was a fixture on the defense and the return team. I couldn't have been more excited and pleased. I was playing the perfect position for my skill set, and I was gaining attention nationally, especially within the Western Athletic Conference, which UNM belonged to at the time. On the football field at UNM, much like at North High, I felt like everything was clicking.

Spiritually, things were starting to click as well. I was continuing to grow in my faith—attending Bible studies, reading books, and going to conferences and seminars on campus that were led by well-known

Bible scholars such as Hal Lindsey. My knowledge of Christianity was deepening. But had it permeated my heart?

After Coach Feldman led us to a 3–8 and 4–7 record my first two seasons, Bill Mondt, our offensive coordinator who had initially recruited me when I was in high school, took over as head coach my junior season.

On a personal level, I knew how important my junior season would be for my future. That's because most NFL scouts do their scouting on juniors so that they have players on their radar by the time they are seniors. And though I was a young college junior, I knew this much: I *wanted* to play in the NFL. It was my dream.

My junior season, however, ended up being a slight step backward.

Our defensive backs coach who had helped me so much the previous year was no longer my coach, and a young guy who had just won a national championship with the Nebraska Cornhuskers a couple years before had joined the UNM staff to coach the defensive backs. For whatever reason, he didn't like me. I'm not sure if he wanted to develop his own recruits or what, but if he had had it his way, he would have started someone else instead of me. I still led the team with four interceptions in 1974, but my involvement on the defense was an obvious step backward from the year before.

> *"My inability to venture through life without a romantic partner became a massive character flaw. Though I was a Christian, it was as if I was always searching for something that could affirm my worth or convince me that I was whole."*

The same was also true for me spiritually and personally. Though I continued to grow and learn more than ever before, I found it difficult to change some of my old habits. I was still unknowingly insecure, which is probably why I ended up in another unhealthy physical relationship—again searching for affection.

My inability to venture through life without a romantic partner became a massive character flaw.

Though I was a Christian, it was as if I was always searching for something that could affirm my worth or convince me that I was whole. And I always thought that my performance in football or in a romantic relationship could fill the void in my heart.

What's interesting about my search for love and acceptance, however, was that in college, I finally started identifying the type of relationship that I wanted. For perhaps the first time, I felt guilty for some of my actions in my romantic relationships. I felt convicted that my choices were not healthy or godly.

I realized that I wanted a relationship that was different than anything I had ever had. A relationship that was built on something beyond physical attraction: something that was built on faith, commitment, fellowship, and friendship.

Things got back on track for me my senior year, both on the field and off the field.

On the field, in 1975, I ended up racking up 324 return yards, a record that stood until the year 2000 when my nephew, Chad Smith, broke that record. (That was a special moment that I had the privilege of witnessing from the sidelines. I can still see my nephew receiving the punt, cutting diagonally across the field, and sprinting by me on the sideline as I trailed him and cheered him on. After scoring a touchdown, he ran straight to the sidelines and gave me a hug. That was the best moment I ever experienced on the field at the University of New Mexico.)

My senior year, I led the team with six interceptions on the season, and I set the university record with fifteen career interceptions (a record that record still stands today). I also received All-Conference honors and again received the Colonel H.J. Golightly Defensive MVP award for the Lobos.

When it came to my dream of playing in the NFL, something that benefited me was that we had one of the best quarterbacks in the country on our team: Steve Myer, who would go onto play four seasons in the NFL with the Seattle Seahawks. Luckily for me, a lot of scouts visited UNM to watch Steve, so they also caught a glimpse of me.

After losing more than half of our games the year before, Coach

Mondt led us to a 6–5 record my senior year—the first winning season for the Lobos since 1971.

The highlight of my senior season was a huge victory on the road against our rival, the University of Arizona, who was ranked No. 13 in the country at the time. We beat them 44–34, our first win against them in five years, bringing the famous Kit Carson Rifle back to Albuquerque. Another interesting thing about that game was that I once again faced one of my hometown rivals, Theopolis Bell, who had played running back at Bakersfield High and played wide receiver for Arizona. Theopolis and I faced one another at every single level of the game.

The Lobos didn't win another game against a ranked team on the road until 2003.

Off the field, things got even better my senior year.

I had started dating a girl from Dallas immediately after my junior season in the spring, and never before in my life had I fallen for someone like that. I'll call her Cindy. One of my mentors from Campus Crusade, who Cindy's family supported financially, had introduced us. Cindy was intelligent, beautiful, and a strong Christian woman. And we were in love.

This also happened to be the only Christian relationship I had ever really been in. We had our spiritual priorities in place—which included purity, studying the Word, and attending church together. It was amazing to be in a relationship that was based on friendship and connection, not lust. Cindy gave me a kind of affection, a kind of love, that I never even knew that I could have—a deep one, one that was rooted in God.

I wanted to spend the rest of my life with her.

It seemed like I had found the right one.

My senior year, I bought an engagement ring in November and planned to ask her parents for permission over Thanksgiving break. And as I neared the end of my senior season in football, I was excited about what the future might hold.

I had a newfound faith, had stumbled upon the girl of my dreams, and hoped that I might get drafted into the NFL.

Things were going great.

My time in Albuquerque were some of the most shaping years of my life when it came to deep concepts like faith and relationships.

I WAS UNAWARE, however, that beneath the surface, a spiritual paradigm that I call "Capitalistic Christianity" was forming. This is a paradigm that I believe the church in America needs to be aware of because of the damage it can cause. Let me explain.

I believed that I was saved by grace (Ephesians 2:8) and that God's grace was sufficient for me (2 Corinthians 12:9), but I thought the sanctification process hinged on my works. I approached my spirituality much like I approached the sport of football, which is why I have paralleled life and football in this chapter. In other words, I thought I was only as good as my performance. I thought my worth was determined by what I did or did not do. When Dan first started to disciple me, I might as well have said to him, "Explain to me the game, and don't change the strategy. Give me the playbook, and don't change the rules at halftime."

For example, in football, one thing that I remember about our huge win against the University of Arizona my senior year was walking off the field with Coach Mondt at the end of the game. He had the prized musket in one hand, and he put his other arm around me and said, "Great game, Randy."

> "In other words, I thought I was only as good as my performance. I thought my worth was determined by what I did or did not do."

"No, Coach," I told him, "I didn't have that great of a game. But I promise you it's going to be better next week."

That shows you how ultracritical of my performance I had become. When your performance masks your insecurities, you wear it like a nice suit and tie. And my spirituality was no different. I was ultracritical of myself and sometimes robbed my Christian life of enjoyment because my identity was in what I did, not in who God said I was.

Similarly, I once heard a modern parable about a drug addict who responded to a pastor's sermon about salvation by kneeling at the altar. After the church service, the drug addict, excited to have freedom in Christ and the assurance that he would spend eternity in heaven, said to the pastor, "I've been a drug user, and I am excited to be a Christian." The pastor, out of the goodness of his heart, gave the addict some discipleship material—a Bible and a supplemental book about the Christian life.

The next week, the addict approached the pastor and said, "I kicked the hard drugs, but I just can't get away from the marijuana." The pastor, out of the goodness of his heart, said to him, "Well, here are some Scripture verses to remember, and I'd like for you to get involved in a Bible study group."

The following week, the addict approached the pastor and said the same thing. Out of the goodness of his heart, the pastor said, "Have you been memorizing those verses I gave you? Have you been going to the small group I suggested? By the way, we also have a parking lot ministry. Have you ever thought about getting involved in that?"

A year went by, and the addict, though desperately trying to change, struggled to rid himself of the drugs entirely. The pastor, frustrated with his inability to cure the man of his addiction, gave up on him. The man, overcome with guilt and shame, left the church and abandoned the Christian faith entirely.

Both the pastor and the addict based their success off their spiritual performance: the pastor in his ability or inability to fix the man and the man in his ability or inability to rid himself of his drug addiction.

I believe that this is a tendency for a lot of us. Why? Because we are taught in our culture to perform. We are taught formulas: *If you do this, this, and this, you get this.* We are raised in a culture that teaches us there is a cause and effect.

Want to see results on the field? *Work hard.*

Want a promotion at work? *Work hard.*

Want the American dream? *Work hard.*

Toil beneath the sun, and then you reap the benefits. But that's not the Christian life.

I did not yet realize that attaining fulfillment in the Christian life was unlike anything else in this world. I thought that I could work my way into God's favor—just as I had worked my way as an underdog into the top level of college football and just as I hoped to one day work my way into the NFL.

My performance-based mentality—on and off the football field— hadn't yet led to an identity crisis. But one day, it would.

Elevating Performance

- How have your experiences and culture affected the way you approach your faith? Can you relate at all to performance-based spirituality or "Capitalistic Christianity"? Why or why not?

- Do you feel like your spiritual performance affects God's opinion of you? Why or why not?

- Read Romans 5:8, 1 Corinthians 6:19, Galatians 3:26, Ephesians 2:10, and 1 John 1:9. What does God say about you?

CHAPTER 7

The Long Road Back from Dallas

Driving to Dallas, Texas, I was excited and extremely nervous.

It was the week of Thanksgiving, and I was going to spend the long weekend with my girlfriend Cindy and her family. I was planning on asking her parents for permission to marry their daughter.

I knew that Cindy's family was wealthy, but I didn't realize how wealthy until I pulled onto their property in North Dallas and started making my way down their long driveway with its overhanging trees. Then I saw their gigantic house in the distance. There I was—a Dalian and 08er—planning on asking the owners of *that* house for their daughter's hand in marriage!

I had met my girlfriend's family a couple of times in Albuquerque. In fact, the week before, her parents had met my parents at the University of New Mexico's annual homecoming game. I had provided all of them with tickets. It turned out to be a great game, and I even returned a punt for a touchdown. I can only imagine what kind of raucous my mom was making on that play. (People had always told me that my mother was loud and crazy during my football games.)

My second day with Cindy's family in Dallas, while we were all eating dinner, I brought up my intentions with Cindy and our future. (By the way, Cindy was fully aware of the plan.)

When I brought up our future, her parents asked me a lot of important questions, but they also asked me some questions that left me a bit confused. For example, they asked, "Did you know that our daughter likes shoes?" I was baffled by what they meant.

Then they asked the big question: "Have you purchased the ring yet?"

I told them that I had purchased the ring and excused myself from the table to retrieve the diamond ring from my suitcase upstairs. I was anxious and excited to show the engagement ring to them. When I returned to the table and showed them the ring, however, they responded with a deflated, "Oh…"

I'm not sure what caused their reaction. Perhaps they didn't like that I had already purchased the ring, assuming they would say yes. Perhaps there was something about me they didn't like. Or perhaps they didn't like the ring I had purchased.

"How do you plan on taking care of the two of you after college?" Cindy's dad asked.

"Well, I'm hoping to play in the NFL, but I am also considering a life in ministry work," I mentioned.

"People in ministry don't make much money," her father responded.

I knew that. They knew that. After all, my mentor, who they supported financially through Campus Crusade, had introduced me to their daughter.

"We'll talk about it," her father eventually said.

As awkward as the exchange was, my girlfriend and I were happy that we'd had the conversation with her parents and had put our future marriage into motion. We went on a date afterwards and then returned to her parents' house.

The next morning, a knock on my door woke me from my sleep. It was extremely early.

"Hello?" I questioned.

"It's me," Cindy said.

"Just a minute," I responded, sitting up.

As she stepped into my room, I noticed that her eyes were puffy and her face was marked by exhaustion. It looked like she had been up all night.

"What's the matter?" I asked.

The first thing she said to me was, "I don't think it's going to work."

"What are you talking about?"

"They said no," she told me, getting to the point. "This isn't going to work out, and my parents think it is best that you leave."

My heart sunk. My mind was racing. I couldn't figure out what had gone wrong.

I eventually realized that there was no way for me to fight this with her parents, so I quietly packed my bags and moseyed through the house with my things, walking out the back door where my car was parked. Awkwardly, Cindy and her parents followed me outside. Before I left, her father said to me, "It might not make sense to you right now, but in time you'll understand that this is the right decision."

"No," I said respectfully and plainly. "I love your daughter. This just doesn't seem right."

And then I left.

As I made the shameful trip home, I thought to myself, *Lord, this is going to be a hard one for me to trust you with.*

And I couldn't help but think about the dinky ring in my pocket.

I WAS UNAWARE that my insecurity and the aching feeling that I wasn't enough had popped up again. I was frustrated.

For the first time, I'd thought I was in the right relationship, but I had seemingly failed, and that made me angry. It shattered my confidence. It bruised my faith. Each time I made a decision to proceed deeper down the path of faith, I seemed to be met by something traumatic. After accepting Christ, I was confronted by Mark's death. After four years of growth and deciding that I might like to pursue ministry, I was confronted with heartbreak and rejection.

Since my childhood—when my absent and angry father had left a void of approval and affection in my life—I'd been scrambling around trying to find someone (a girlfriend) or something (football) to convince me that I was enough. In reflection, I can see that this void was very real. And when these avenues led to disappointment or didn't meet my expectations, it was hard and painful.

> *"The human experience is comprised of a multitude of voids—the general feeling that there is something missing—and we can either let God into those voids or we can try to take control ourselves."*

Such an occurrence is natural when you elevate something of this world above God. Looking back, it's obvious to me that there was a void in my life that I had not allowed God to fill. The human experience is comprised of a multitude of voids—the general feeling that there is something missing—and we can either let God into those voids or we can try to take control ourselves.

I was a young Christian living a performance-based life. I knew very little about surrender, because that equation stripped me of control. We must surrender our voids to God as we become aware of them.

Of course, thanks to Dan, I learned a lot about my Christian faith at this point in time, which was indeed an anchor of hope for me. But I was yet to become aware of the insecurities within me. My Christianity was transforming how I saw the world, but it had not yet transformed how I saw myself or all that I had experienced in my past. It was transforming my mind but not necessarily my heart.

"The reality is that your insecurities will always return. The key is: how will you react when they do return? The authenticity of a Christian is determined by how he or she reacts to adversity."

Looking back, I wish I had been aware of my desperate search to be enough.

Today, when these feelings or insecurities return, I can recognize them as if they are old friends and can handle their presence appropriately. I hope I succeed more often than not in confronting them, but I know that I still fail. I can usually combat the lies that my insecurities are whispering to me with truths that I believe.

The reality is that your insecurities will *always* return. The key is: how will you react when they do return?

The authenticity of a Christian is determined by how he or she reacts to adversity. How someone reacts to difficult situations reveals the depths of that person's character.

Today, I'm not too proud to say, "I didn't handle that well." Then, however, I knew nothing about introspection. I was merely existing, reacting in an unhealthy way whenever my pursuits failed to fill the void.

I didn't know it at the time, but the way I reacted to my insecurities would eventually get me into trouble and lead to the biggest mistake of my life.

The Universal Search for "Enough-ness"

- The tendency to place our identities and worth in the things of this world is a universal struggle. What do you use to convince yourself of your "enough-ness"?

- What makes you feel that you are not enough? Your upbringing? Your socioeconomic status? Rejection? Shame? Try to target the direct lie beneath the surface that haunts you and taunts you. Example: "I often feel like I am not enough because __________."

- Read 1 Peter 2:9. What does God say about your enough-ness? What does God say about your mission in this life?

- How can you combat the lies that your insecurities are whispering with truths that you believe?

CHAPTER 8
Nothing Wasted

I was a wreck the following semester.

When we returned to school, Cindy and I still secretively spent time together and even talked once about the possibility of eloping. But I believe that both of us, deep down inside, knew that eloping wasn't the right thing to do. Her parents, who found out that we were still pursuing the relationship, eventually moved her to North Carolina to live with family friends, as if to quarantine her. Cindy and I never spoke again.

Truth is, Cindy always trusted that the Lord would use her parents to confirm who she would spend her life with—and I'm sure that's how it ended up. I hope she's had a wonderful life. I've always wanted nothing but the best for her.

As heartbroken as I was, I knew that I had to get a move on with my life. There was nothing I could do. Her parents had all the power and all the resources to make it impossible for us to remain together. It was hard to get through the semester.

On top of my messed-up love life, I knew I wouldn't be graduating with my class because I was a few credits short of my college degree. I'd have to return sometime down the road to finish up school and collect my degree.

Though I was struggling in school and in my personal life, I knew that the NFL Draft was on the horizon. I continued to dedicate myself to training and lifting throughout the semester. Football once again became an outlet for me to release all my anger from my unprocessed pain.

When our insecurities resurface, it seems that our outlets resurface as well. Sometimes they can be healthy escapes; sometimes they can be ways for us to run from our problems. Football, at different times in my life, was both.

It was during this time that I once again saw the labels return—that I was "too small" and "too slow" and "just not good enough" to play at the next level. But I had done all that I needed to do at the University of New Mexico, capping off my career with All-WAC honors and multiple WAC Defensive Player of the Week honors. Some people even started to call me an anomaly.

> *"When our insecurities resurface, it seems that our outlets resurface as well. Sometimes they can be healthy escapes; sometimes they can be ways for us to run from our problems. Football, at different times in my life, was both."*

In January or February, several scouts from the Denver Broncos swung through Albuquerque and said that there was a good chance that they would select me in the 1976 NFL Draft. It was fitting for the Broncos to say such a thing since they had a Californian cornerback out of the University of Washington named Calvin Jones who was only five feet seven and weighed 170 pounds.

I couldn't believe that an NFL team would say they would draft *me*.

While working out throughout the winter and the spring, I knew my future was in the hands of the Lord. I hoped that the scout from the Broncos meant what he had told me—that they would draft me. I was on the brink of attaining my dream.

But then the first day of the NFL Draft, April 8, came and went. Nothing.

And then the second day of the draft, April 9, came and went. Nothing.

That haunting word—*undrafted*—had become my reality.

What disappointed me most during the draft was that I saw guys I had played against in the WAC—guys who did not have the college accolades that I had—get drafted into the NFL. There was a defensive back from Wyoming, for example, who was drafted in the first round by the Dallas Cowboys. When he was selected, I thought, *Wow, things are looking good for me.*

I couldn't figure it out. Was this the end of my football career?

I think for anyone who has played a sport or done something for a long time, he or she is eventually confronted with the reality of this statement: *What will I do if I can no longer do that thing?*

Two months passed in no man's land, and I eventually received another call from the Broncos. This time, they invited me to a trial. (The Broncos likely understood during the draft that I wasn't on the radar of any other NFL team, so they decided not to waste a pick on me since they knew they could invite me to a trial.)

I inked a two-thousand-dollar signing bonus and reported to trial camp in the spring…with twenty-seven other defensive backs. That's right. *Twenty-seven.*

I survived trial camp and was one of twelve defensive backs to advance to training camp. They were only going to keep seven.

Considering I had begun as a seventh-string safety, I knew that this was the road less traveled—which was also the road of opportunity. Getting drafted would have felt much more secure, because I would have known the organization had used their pick on me. I felt no security, but I also knew that this was my chance.

I had a great showing at training camp and made the preseason roster.

Next I had to prove myself in the actual preseason games.

I played well—well enough to make it all the way to the final cut heading into our final preseason game.

Head coach John Ralston told us that there were three of us—me, Chris Pane, and Steve Foley—fighting for the last two spots. And the decision, he told us, would be made based on our performance in the final preseason game.

Since the game was in Denver, my parents decided to make the fifteen-hour drive from Bakersfield to watch me. My mom and dad had a much different relationship by this point in my life—infinitely more tranquil than the abusive one they'd had in my childhood. My relationship with my father, though it still lacked depth and normalcy, also seemed to be more stable.

I'm glad they came, too, because I had a pretty good game.

I made a number of tackles and even caused a fumble while playing special teams on punt coverage that led to a game-winning touchdown. I can only imagine what my mother was doing in the stands.

Chris Pane had an okay game, but it wasn't anything special.

Steve Foley had the worst game out of the three of us. I hated that for Steve because, though I was competing against him, he was one of my dear friends and still is.

"You're in, Randy," Steve said to me after the game, acknowledging that I had outplayed both him and Chris. "Man, you had the better game."

I went to bed that night full of confidence that I had made the Denver Broncos regular season roster.

The next morning, our day off, I took my parents to Rocky Mountain National Park to celebrate our victory and my performance from the night before. I remember feeling accomplished and being excited for the future. Ever since I'd been brought into training camp as a seventh-string safety, I'd done everything that I needed to do to make the team—all the way to the final preseason game.

While we were at the park, Steve received a call from Coach Ralston, asking him to meet at his office at the facility. (I only know the following exchange because of what Steve has shared with me. Obviously, at the time, I had no idea this meeting took place.)

When Steve sat down in Coach Ralston's office, Coach said, "Steve, you didn't have a good game yesterday. What's up?"

"I know," Steve said. "I'm the guy you need to cut."

"No, Steve," Coach Ralston replied. "We believe in you, and we are going to keep you. I just want you to know that we believe in you." (Of course, this ultimately ended up being not only a good decision but a *brilliant* decision by the Broncos, as Steve went on to play for the Broncos for the next decade and become the franchise's all-time leader in interceptions.)

Steve was in.

Unbeknownst to me at the time, the decision was between me and Chris.

When I returned from the park to my hotel room with my parents, I noticed that my hotel phone was blinking. I had a voice message from the Broncos organization asking me to call them back when I got a chance.

I immediately called them, and the director of player personnel, who we players called the "Hatchet Man" for obvious reasons, said to me, "Hey, Randy, you need to come on over to the facility to meet with Coach Ralston. Bring your playbook."

My heart sunk.

When you are told to bring your playbook, it doesn't mean that the coaches are going to sit there and go over plays with you. It only means one thing: that you are getting cut. This was the end.

I didn't understand. I was confused. I had performed better than both Steve Foley *and* Chris Pane.

My mind was suddenly bombarded with thoughts. I once again began asking myself questions that were rooted in the lie: was I good enough?

This was just one more circumstance in a difficult phase of my life that was filled with rejection. The two avenues in my life where I had always gone searching for approval and affection—football and romance—seemed to be collapsing beneath my feet. I wish I had realized at the time that I was being presented with an opportunity to find my worth in something much, much deeper. But I didn't.

I went to the team training facility and sat down with Coach Ralston, and it became apparent to me that he had decided to go with Steve and Chris—not because of our performances the night before, as Coach Ralston had said would be the determining factor, but because of their previous experience. They had both spent a year playing in the defunct World Football League, and the head coach said that experience was appealing to the coaching staff.

I handed Coach Ralston my playbook.

What's interesting is that, as I drove back to Bakersfield with my parents, I had the sweetest time that I had ever had with my mom and dad. I was in a delicate state, not knowing what I was doing or where I was going to go, a situation that I had never really been in before.

My dad, for the first time, demonstrated a sensitivity to what was going on in my life. He even told me that he loved me. He was angry that I got cut after playing so well in the final preseason game, but his anger was in my defense.

It took us two days to drive from Denver to California, so we took

> *"I didn't realize it at the time, but the moment was a foreshadowing for what would become a major theme in my life: finding beauty and blessing in brokenness."*

our time and tried to enjoy it together. As I grieved my latest disappointment and processed the most recent wave of rejection, Mom and Dad said everything that I would've wanted them to say. It was great. We had a moment, as they say.

Some things, like my childhood, were too messy to ever fully repair, but on that drive back to Bakersfield, some of that seemed to be redeemed. I didn't realize it at the time, but the moment was a foreshadowing for what would become a major theme in my life: finding beauty and blessing in brokenness.

I WAS UNAWARE at the time that an important mindset when encountering frustration or disappointment is to look for potential redemptive elements. It's interesting how that sometimes works—how life's most difficult, uncontrollable moments, how its most fragile and vulnerable circumstances can lead to something sweet and redemptive, like my car ride home with my parents. Suffering can take us deeper into who we really are as God's beloved children—without attachments, without avenues, and without outlets. It can force us to find meaning in different ways. In our challenges, we are presented with an opportunity to apply our faith—to believe that God works in our struggles for the good of those who love Him, to believe that there is nothing wasted in God's economy.

Viktor Frankl, a Holocaust survivor and author of *Man's Search for Meaning*, says that one way to experience meaning is to discover redemptive elements in our sufferings. While this does not explain the suffering, it can help us find meaning either after or during the current storm. It can help us realize that *nothing in our lives is wasted.*

The question is not whether we will face disappointments, which can best be defined as unmet expectations, in this life. The real questions should be: What do I do with disappointments? Am I willing to ask myself the hard questions? What does rejection reveal about my blind spots and insecurities? Am I willing to let God fill those voids, whatever they might be?

Disappointment often propels us into a new realm of faith and understanding. Disappointment is often the catalyst to unexpected blessings.

Later in my life, I listened to an audio series by pastor Charles Stanley titled *Brokenness: The Way to Blessing*. It's a series I highly recommend. Dr. Stanley also wrote a book titled *The Blessings of Brokenness*, which is also very good and is in the same vein of his audio series. Stanley's work helped me to see that brokenness is where true growth and transformation takes place—how it often opens the door for blessing.

> *"In our challenges, we are presented with an opportunity to apply our faith—to believe that God works in our struggles for the good of those who love Him, to believe that there is nothing wasted in God's economy."*

But it is sometimes difficult to see that brokenness can lead to blessing because our biggest disappointments usually take place in areas of our lives that are closest to our hearts—which, in my case, were relationships and football. This makes it especially difficult to find something redemptive in our disappointments, because these are the areas that we often try to control and micromanage.

This was certainly true for me. Redemption, in my mind, could only be found by somehow pulling myself up by my bootstraps and excelling on the football field. In chasing my dream of playing in the NFL, I was more focused than ever. But I was also very miserable—even though I had just had one of the best moments I had ever experienced with my mom and dad.

Redemptive Elements of Suffering

- Many of the discussion questions at the end of each chapter have dealt with becoming aware of insecurities. This journey of awareness can sometimes be painful. What are some redemptive elements of this difficult journey?

- How have your past sufferings helped you to meet others where they are at and encourage them in their own sufferings? How might you be able to use your current sufferings to encourage others in the future?

- Read James 1:2–8. What stands out to you about this passage?

CHAPTER 9
When Your Boss Doesn't Like You

When I was cut from the Broncos, it was too late for me to reenroll in class at the University of New Mexico, so I went to Oregon to work with my brother, Roger, in his construction business. I worked there throughout the first semester and reenrolled in class the second semester.

As I worked with Roger throughout the fall and winter, I couldn't help but once again wonder if my NFL journey had come to an end. I did not receive a call from an NFL team during the regular season. Nor did I have any inclination whatsoever that any NFL teams had me on their radar. I was history to them.

But I also didn't feel as if it was time to move on. I didn't feel like I was ready to forfeit my dream. If there was one thing that my experience in Denver taught me, it was this: *I could play.* I could hold my own in the NFL.

So I kept working out while I was in Oregon with my brother, knowing that if I received a call, I wanted to be in as good of shape as possible. I worked out as though I might get a call any day. But as the weeks passed, I realized that was not going to happen.

Christmas came, the regular season ended, and I *still* hadn't received any encouraging news.

I decided to reenroll at the University of New Mexico to complete my final semester and to continue working out with my former coaches and teammates. It was there that I met someone—a sweet, beautiful woman who had been the runner-up for Miss New Mexico the year before. We began to date. Looking back, I wasn't ready for a relationship considering how my previous relationship had traumatically fallen apart, but I did not want to be alone and was honestly afraid that I wouldn't find anyone else. I wasn't trusting God. I rushed into it.

But while I was at UNM, my NFL dreams were resurrected from the dead.

Enter: Detroit Lions head coach Tommy Hudspeth.

Coach Hudspeth's son, Max, was a highly recruited player coming out of high school. When he visited UNM my sophomore year (his senior year in high school), I actually hosted him as a recruit. We ended up being roommates his freshman year and my junior year. Because of this personal connection, Coach Hudspeth had an understanding of what I could do and what I might be able to offer an NFL organization.

I received a call from Coach Hudspeth in February, offering me a free-agent contract with the Lions in the spring. I completed my Bachelor of University Studies degree (with an emphasis on biology), and, though it was a degree that I would never use, it was an accomplishment for a kid from little Oildale. And then I reported to mini-camp in May.

I went to the Lions with new life and new hope. It was a great feeling knowing that there was a coach who knew about me and understood what I was capable of on the field. You see, scouting back then was not as sophisticated and comprehensive as it is today. Nowadays, there are videos and statistics and all kinds of ways for recruits to be discovered through the Internet. Back then, however, it was all word-of-mouth.

Interestingly, another coach for the Lions that season was none other than Bill Belichick—yes, *the* Bill Belichick who has five Super Bowl rings. Back in 1977, when Belichick was getting his coaching start in the NFL, he was a special teams coach for the Lions and was often ordered around by the other coaches. He was just getting his feet wet at the time—getting acclimated to the coaching profession. Once, however, I remember standing next to Coach Belichick during practice while a teammate of mine smarted off to one of the coaches. Coach Belichick leaned over to me and said, "If I was the coach, I'd kick his butt out of here."

Throughout preseason, Detroit felt like a good fit for me. My coaches made me the primary returner for punts and kickoffs. I lit up the board, ranking in the Top 5 in the NFC in kick returns and punt returns during those exhibition games. After each preseason game, more and more of the media seemed to be gathering around me in the locker room, as they were drawn to the typical underdog story. This is one of the neat things about preseason football. Several storylines emerge about unknown players who have a chance of making the team and fulfilling their dreams.

But then the story took an even crazier turn.

In our pregame workout right before our final preseason game, I remember crowding around defensive backs coach Burnie Miller—a great coach who happened to starkly resemble comedian Jackie Gleason—and listening to him announce the starters for the game, as was the routine. What's interesting about the last game of the preseason is that the projected regular season starters play more than in any other game in order to get loose and gain some momentum heading into the regular season. I was yet to start at the defensive back position. This was understandable since I was behind Charlie West, an All-Pro safety, and Lem Barney, a future Pro Football Hall of Famer—two names that are etched in NFL history.

But that's when Coach Burnie, reading from his sheet, uttered the words: "Strong safety: Rich."

I had no idea what it was all about. I was shocked.

Of all the games Coach Burnie might have had me start as a defensive back, the *final* preseason game—when fans and media typically get a glimpse of the regular season roster and starters—was the last game I expected to start.

Inside, the nerves ignited me. The anxiousness. The anticipation. It was almost overwhelming. I had been given an opportunity to demonstrate that I was capable of making the team.

My work was cut out for me, however. Our opponent, the Cleveland Browns, were a good team, and I would be mostly covering six-foot-six tight end Oscar Roan—a tough matchup for someone who stood at five feet nine.

Turns out, I ended up having a *great* performance. I played the entire game, still assuming my normal role on special teams, and I held my own covering Roan.

After the game, the media surrounded me in the locker room. Apparently they understood the significance of me starting at strong safety. They bombarded me with questions:

"What are your chances of making the team?"

"How did you end up starting?"

I spoke up above all of them and said, "Look, if God wants me here, I'll be here."

The headline in the *Detroit Free Press* read something along the lines of: "Rich Says if God Wants Him Here, He'll Be Here."

Not a smart thing to say when your general manager, Russ Thomas, isn't a believer.

At the start of our next practice, I waited on the football field with my teammates, but none of the coaches were there.

Ten minutes went by. No coaches.

Twenty minutes. No coaches.

Thirty minutes. No coaches.

Finally, after about forty-five minutes, they emerged from the facility and walked onto the practice field. Coach Burnie approached one of the defensive backs named Benny and said to him, "Coach Hudspeth needs to talk to you. Bring your playbook."

I felt horribly for Benny, but just like that, I was on the team.

I had done it.

After the frustrations of the previous year—all the rejection, all the false promises, all the confusion—I had made an NFL team. After getting cut the year before and seemingly fading into oblivion, my dream was still intact.

Our first regular season game was against the Chicago Bears at Soldier Field in Chicago.

Once again, I played well. Not only did I return punts and kicks; I also got on the field as a defensive back. This happened to feature a physical encounter with the great Walter Payton, who I consider to be the best running back to ever play the game.

I was sent in on a nickel package—meaning five defensive backs—to play deep safety because the coaches suspected that the Bears were going to run a passing play. Well, the Bears *didn't* run a passing play. Instead, they ran a disguised sweep to Walter Payton to my left, and no one was there to tackle him. Walter exploded up the field, going full speed, and I was forced to come all the way up out of my coverage zone to attempt an open-field tackle on the best halfback in the game.

I sprinted after him, lunged toward him, and—*BAM*—slammed right into him.

Though I had indeed made the tackle, I had neglected one of the most fundamental rules for a tackler in football: keeping my head on the front side of the running back. I don't know if Walter put on a good move or if I closed my eyes, but I made the tackle incorrectly. I like to think he put a good move on me because I don't want to think that I closed my eyes.

Nonetheless, there I was, lying flat on the ground, unable to get up. I wasn't knocked out, but I was dizzy. My teammates later told me that Walter got right back up and returned to the huddle. Of course he did.

A trainer came over and looked at me and said, "Are you okay?" I couldn't see clearly out of my left eye. Honestly, I thought my eyeball had popped out.

My world was spinning.

My shoulder was in pain.

Welcome to the NFL.

There's nothing like getting run over by Walter Payton in your first regular season game.

Our trainer straightened my helmet, and—what do you know—I could see again. My eye hadn't popped out after all; my helmet was merely cockeyed.

After regaining my composure, I slowly made my way off the field and then stood on the sidelines at Soldier Stadium, as their fans began to yell at me.

"What's the matter, you can't take a hit?"

"You're too small to play in this league!"

"Nice try, you wimp!"

Most of the other things they said, I can't repeat in this book. The truth is that they were pouring it on. And for a moment, I'll admit that I started listening to the crowd.

But then it dawned on me: *Why would I listen to people sitting in the stands who could only dream and fantasize about playing in an NFL game?* As author Max Lucado once wrote, "A man who wants to lead the orchestra must turn his back on the crowd."

I eventually turned around, looked at the crowd, smiled and waved to them. For one of the first times, I discovered that the bullies—known to some youth today as "haters"—will continue to pour it on as long as they know they are getting to you. When I waved and smiled, they just shut up.

I tell kids that I speak to today that what haters want to do is steal your dreams. Haters are usually people with strong insecurities who want to bring you down and pull you back. But you can't listen to the crowd. As cliché as it might sound, you have to follow your heart. And dreams are birthed inside your heart.

> *"The truth is that bad choices in life have nothing to do with who you are— they are simply a result of having your head on the wrong side."*

When I went into the locker room at halftime, my shoulder was in a lot of pain, and I felt like I was confronted with the question: "Am I big enough to play this game?"

But as I sat there and thought about it, I realized that it had nothing to do with my size. Rather, it had everything to do with my head. See, you *always* tackle with your head on the front side of the body, which I didn't do when I tackled Walter Payton.

The truth is that bad choices in life have nothing to do with who you are—they are simply a result of having your head on the wrong side. And sometimes those bad choices can hurt. I decided in the locker room that if I got back out there on the field, I needed to keep my head on the right side.

Bad choices happen in life. But it's important to step back, remove yourself from the situation, and get your head on the right side again.

So, despite the somewhat embarrassing wakeup call that I received in my first regular-season game in the NFL, I decided that it was all part of the process and that nothing would deter me from following my dream. Not to mention, I'd still made the tackle on Walter Payton, possibly prevented a touchdown, and played a solid game on special teams.

Though I played well against the Bears, our next game—at home against the New Orleans Saints—turned out to be a personal debacle.

On one play while on the punt coverage unit, I was playing the role of the "gunner"—the outside guy whose job is to get down the field first and force the returner to quickly decide what he is going to do, whether to call a fair catch or field the return. When the ball was punted, I started counting in my head, knowing that most punts usually have 3.8 to 4 seconds of hang time. However, this punt was a short and high kick, and I ended up hitting the returner before he even caught the ball.

I was called for a penalty, and when I got to the sideline, Coach Hudspeth was in my ear yelling, "What in the world were you doing?!"

On another play, I was on punt coverage and was supposed to block inside and out. The guy I was supposed to block juked me big time and blocked the punt. I got chewed out for that mistake, too.

The next day, our day off, someone from player personnel gave me a call and said, "Randy, I hate making this call, but come on in. Coach Hudspeth needs to talk to you…and bring your playbook."

I knew what that meant.

When I arrived at the facility, one of my friends on the team, a backup quarterback named Joe Reed, was just leaving a quarterbacks' meeting when he saw me. He asked what I was doing there since quarterbacks were the only players meeting on our day off. I told him I had gotten "the call."

After some heartfelt conversation, Joe jokingly made the comment, "Don't worry, Randy. Detroit cuts a guy every year, and he ends up playing in the Super Bowl." (Apparently this had happened the last several years.)

I forced a laugh and then ran into Coach Burnie, my defensive backs coach. "Randy, this isn't right," he vented. "Management here needs to let us keep the team that we want. I'm sorry about this; there's nothing we can do."

I then entered Coach Hudspeth's office, and he, too, empathized with me in my situation.

"Randy," he said, "remember a couple weeks ago when we coaches didn't come out to practice for a while? Well, we were all in front of Russ Thomas defending our choice to keep you on the team. He doesn't like you, and it might have something to do with what you said in the newspaper article about God. I can't do anything about it."

As I look back, I don't regret testifying that I believed God was in control of my life. I was just being myself, and I felt like the opportunity to play for the Lions had truly come from the Lord.

There are going to be times in our lives that we need to testify what we believe regardless of what the consequences might be. We shouldn't shy away from who we really are.

After going up to Canada for four or five days to test out the Canadian Football League with the Calgary Stampeders (turns out I didn't like the CFL), I received a call from the head of player personnel with the Denver Broncos. They wanted to pay me five hundred dollars a week to be part of their unofficial scout team—a handful of guys who would practice with the team and attend all the meetings but not dress for the games unless there was an opening or injury in the roster. Obviously, after making the team with the Lions, this was a downgrade. But it was the only opportunity I had to stay connected with an NFL organization, so I went.

When I arrived in Denver, I sat down with the Broncos defensive coordinator Joe Collier. I found it interesting that he was quite up-to-date about what I had done in Detroit and asked what the situation was that had led to me getting released. I told him about my lacking performance in Week 2 and about how Russ Thomas didn't like my quote in the newspaper about God. Coach Collier laughed and didn't seem surprised.

After talking to Coach Collier, I sat down with the newly named head coach Red Miller, who said to me, "We like you, Randy. We are going to add you to the roster whenever we can. Just stick around and continue to prove your worth while playing on the scout team."

But the 1977 Denver Broncos roster was undoubtedly one of the more difficult rosters in the NFL to crack into. When the Broncos acquired me halfway through the season, they were undefeated and had their eyes set on the playoffs, a much different tone than the year before when they finished 9–5 and didn't even make the playoffs. Their success, I felt, could be credited to Coach Miller. He was a players' coach. He was an encourager. I can remember times when he would come into the locker room after practice and practically wrestle with some of the linemen. It seemed like he was "one of the guys," but he still had the respect of every player. I was happy to be a part of a Red Miller team.

The second to last game of the regular season, defensive back Chris Pane (yes, the same guy who beat me out for a spot the year before) blew out his knee.

And, just like that, I was added to the roster.

Our final game of the season was against the Dallas Cowboys in Dallas. This happened to be my first time in Dallas since that shameful and humiliating Thanksgiving two years before when I'd asked my girlfriend's parents for their daughter's hand in marriage. I couldn't help but think about the bad taste I had regarding the Big D. (Unbeknownst to us, we would also end up playing Dallas in the Super Bowl.)

In the Divisional Playoffs, we defeated Chuck Noll's Pittsburgh Steelers, the Super Bowl champions from two years before, 34–21. And in the AFC Championship, we defeated our rival, John Madden's Oakland Raiders, the Super Bowl champions from the year before, 20–17.

We had reached our goal of making it to Super Bowl XII, having defeated the Super Bowl champs from the previous two seasons.

And I was on the roster.

Like my friend Joe Reed had said, "Detroit cuts a guy every year, and he ends up playing in the Super Bowl."

Super Bowl XII was held at the Louisiana Superdome in New Orleans. Although I didn't really feel as if I was truly part of the team, since I had been added to the roster so late in the season, the entire experience was unforgettable.

The week leading up to the Super Bowl, each player was required to sit at a table for at least thirty minutes a day with the media. Today, the players are more quarantined and are simply required to attend Super Bowl Opening Night—a multiple-hour media circus with professionals and non-professionals alike.

Every day, the tables of guys like head coach Red Miller and quarterback Craig Morton were flooded with media personnel. Not many approached a no-name like me. But one day, a reporter from the *Washington Post* said to me, "Randy, I understand there are a lot of Christians on the Denver Broncos team."

"Yes, ma'am," I told her.

"I also understand there are a lot of Christians on the Dallas Cowboys team," she continued. She then paused, looked at me, and said, "So which team do you think God wants to win?"

Ahh, the age-old question: *Does God care who wins?* My big chance for an interview, and she was trying to corner me.

"You know, I don't know that God really cares," I told her. "But I can tell you one thing: in the winning and the losing, God will be glorified by the believers on each team."

She looked at me, got up, closed her notepad, and walked away. She was looking to stir something up. It could have turned out to be an ugly story, but I guess she decided to write about something else.

Another day, a reporter from the *Detroit Free Press* approached my table, asking me how it felt to be a Detroit Lion in the Super Bowl. I told him that I was a Denver Bronco now but was very thankful for the opportunity that Detroit had given me earlier in the season. He wrote a neat story about me in the *Detroit Free Press*.

Overall, the Super Bowl festivities that week were a once-in-a-life-time experience. Unfortunately, we ended up losing to Tom Landry's Cowboys squad 27–10 in Super Bowl XII, but my claim to fame is that I made the first tackle of the game while playing on special teams. I still have an old VHS recording of the game where famous play-by-play announcer Pat Summerall says, "Tackle made by Rrrrrrrandy Rrrrrich!" It's fun to go back and watch it every once in a while. It is a reminder of the wonderful opportunities that God provided for me in the NFL, especially considering where I'd been merely one year before that Super Bowl game, when I thought that my NFL dreams might be finished. But God not only provided me with a route back into the NFL; He also brought me to the best team in the country.

Turns out, I not only had the first tackle in the Super Bowl but also the first penalty. I was playing against Benny Barnes, one of the crafti-est special teams players in the NFL at the time, and as I was running down the field, playing on punt coverage, he kept holding me and covering me. This wasn't the first time he had done this to me, and I was getting sick of it. So I slung my hand into his chest to get him off of me, and it looked like I was trying to start a fight with him.

First tackle. First penalty.

Just trying to make a name for myself.

Oh, yes, one more interesting thing about the Super Bowl....

My new girlfriend and I had become quite an item in a short time, and were already engaged at the time of the Super Bowl. Our plans were to get married during the offseason.

Now I can see that I had a lot more work that I needed to do on myself—yes, before dating her, but *certainly* before getting married. This had nothing to do with her and had everything to do with me. She was a wonderful woman with a sweet spirit—someone who anybody would have been happy to be married to—but my deep wounds and romantic insecurities were unprocessed. How would she have even known this was going on within me? I didn't talk about it with her or with anyone.

That's not to say that I didn't love her—I definitely did—or that the connection that we had was not real—it definitely was. But I rushed into marrying her because I was insecure. *Not* a good reason to get married. Getting married was what everyone else was doing, and it seemed like the right thing to do. Plus, it gave me a companion, which I really wanted. That same old story again: a hurting individual on a search for approval and affection. All along, there were deeper things within me that I wasn't dealing with.

How in the world did I think that I could get married, bring someone else into my life, and try to make her feel secure when I wasn't even secure with who I was myself?

I WAS UNAWARE of how these unrecognized insecurities and my unprocessed shame were leading to rash decision-making in my life. Little did I know at the time that this rash decision-making, especially in my reckless pursuit of affection, would ultimately lead to my life falling apart.

But that's the natural byproduct of unrecognized insecurities and unprocessed shame: knee-jerk reactions. This saying by Socrates is often-quoted but couldn't be more relevant here: "The unexamined life is not worth living." In my case, I was not fully living because I had not dared to examine the scary things in my life that were taking place beneath the surface.

Much the prophet Jonah in the Bible, who constantly reacted to his fears and, in doing so, kept fleeing God's call for him to go to Nineveh and preach, I, too, reacted to my fears and, in doing so, remained out of touch with who I was in Christ.

Throughout my life, I had been afraid of being alone, and so I rushed from relationship to relationship, leaving a trail of destruction along the way. My identity was strapped to outlets like football and romantic relationships by a very strong cord: my fears—fears of not receiving the approval or affection I desired. It seems that fear has a way of doing that: tying your identity to things of this world. I had not yet learned how to say "no" to these worldly passions, as Titus 2:12 says, that were birthed from my fears. Not that getting married was bad in itself. But my hunger for affection was toxic and unhealthy and not fair to my wife. It would later result in me placing unfair expectations upon her.

> *"I guess at the heart of my search were these questions: Would I be okay if my life lacked football, an outlet that brought me approval? Would I be okay if my life lacked a romantic partner, an outlet that brought me affection? What if all I had was the love and grace of God?"*

I guess at the heart of my search were these questions: Would I be okay if my life lacked football, an outlet that brought me approval? Would I be okay if my life lacked a romantic partner, an outlet that brought me affection? What if all I had was the love and grace of God?

I guess that should've been my first sign that I was off-center—that deep down, judging by my recklessness, I didn't know if I'd be okay without these conduits for approval and affection. But at the time I was not mature enough to pose these questions.

Like Jonah, I was enslaved by my own worry and angst, which led to some unexamined, rash decision-making, especially in the arena of affection.

And like Jonah, it would take a storm to get my attention. And a whale to rescue me.

Beneath Our Decisions

- How have unrecognized insecurities or unprocessed shame led you to rash decision-making or poor choices?

- What choices have you made in search for approval and affection?

- Carefully identify your reactions to your insecurities. Are there benefits to these reactions? Are there dangers?

- Read 2 Samuel 11. How did David's ignorance and unawareness of his shame and insecurity lead to rash decision-making?

CHAPTER 10
When What I Did Was Who I Was

My girlfriend and I got married in the early summer of 1978.

Most of my family and best friends were there. Interestingly, my dad was my best man. I don't know how to explain exactly what I was thinking when I selected him. He didn't give me the best model for marriage. But I think it was a reflection of something that I wanted to have with my dad: for us to be *that* close to one another. Looking back, I see it as a vivid demonstration of what I had deeply craved all of my life.

It was a great day, and the next phase of my life began.

The Broncos held onto me in the offseason, but I was once again faced with the same challenge throughout training camp and preseason: making the team.

Though this brought all kinds of stress, I cannot tell you how much I enjoyed being with the Broncos. To this day, the Denver Broncos is the organization that I identify with the most. I was back with so many of my friends from not only the season before but also from two seasons before when I'd been cut from the team. This included my good friend Steve Foley.

Steve was a character and the most even-keeled guy you could ever meet. He was the middle child of thirteen kids, and nothing ever seemed to faze him. Had I been more introspective at the time, I probably could have learned a lot from Steve—like how he didn't take himself or his performance on the football field too seriously.

One day at the beginning of two-a-days, for example, I remember Steve removing a brand new pair of shoes from his locker. He opened the shoebox, paused as if in shock, and in his slow, southern, Louisiana accent said, "Doggone it."

He then pulled out three game checks from the previous season.

"I *thought* I made more money than I had deposited," he laughed.

Another funny story that comes to mind from my time with the Broncos has to do with my teammate Riley Odums, who was one of the first gigantic tight ends in the NFL. He was six feet four inches tall, or something like that, and was an absolute beast of a player. I always used to call him "Big Oak Tree," and he would call me "Little Mesquite Bush."

One time I was sitting next to Riley on a team flight and said to him, "Riley, this is my five-foot-nine advantage." I had plenty of legroom, and Riley's knees were up in his chest. He certainly wasn't as comfortable as I was. The next week at practice, he knocked me on my butt, stood over me, and said, "Randy, this is my six-foot-four advantage."

"Looking back, I can see that the purpose of playing football was about so much more than wins and losses, accumulating stats, and making teams."

What I miss most about football is the camaraderie and friendships—the close relationships I had with my teammates. That's why I like to stay involved with the Denver Broncos Alumni Association as they develop varying community- and veteran-outreach programs. Looking back, I can see that the purpose of playing football was about so much more than wins and losses, accumulating stats, and making teams.

Throughout the preseason, things unfolded nicely with the Broncos.

By the end of the second preseason game, the Broncos had already narrowed the roster down to seven defensive backs, which is how many they had kept in the past. I was looking around, thinking to myself, "Wow, I did it."

A sense of accomplishment washed over me. I knew that nothing would be official until our final preseason game, but things were looking good.

One day at practice heading into our third preseason game, our special teams coach Marv Braden asked me, "Randy, you got married this summer, didn't you?"

"Yeah, Coach, I did," I told him.

"Is she here in Denver with you?" he asked.

"No, she's in Albuquerque. I won't bring her here until after the last cut."

"Randy, we are down to seven defensive backs."

"I know, Coach, but I think I'm going to wait."

The next week at practice heading into our fourth preseason game, we had the same conversation.

"How about that new wife of yours?" Coach Braden prodded. "She up here yet?"

"Nah, Coach, not yet."

"Randy, you need to bring her up."

Toward the end of preseason, I decided to take Coach Braden's advice. I called my wife and told her that one of my coaches felt like it was safe for her to move to Denver for the season. She made the seven-hour trip from Albuquerque, and we planned on beginning our lives together in the Mile High City.

That is, for a few days.

The first practice after our final preseason game, I received a call from Broncos management informing me that, this year only, every team in the NFL had to put three players from their forty-three player roster on waivers within twenty-four hours of their final game. It was a weird rule that the NFL had just implemented. Well, the Broncos hadn't put me on waivers, but they *had* picked up the Oakland Raiders' fourth-round draft pick, a defensive back, thus bumping me off the depth chart. The coaches had no idea that this was my fate. Management was off doing their own thing.

I found myself in Denver with my new wife and wondering where to go.

This is where things get a little crazy.

I received a call the next day from the Minnesota Vikings, inviting me to a two-day trial. So I hopped on a plane and flew to Minneapolis.

That night in my Minneapolis hotel room, I received a call from Steve Ortmayer, head of player personnel for the Oakland Raiders, inviting me to a two-day trial. (By the way, I have no idea how these NFL teams could track your whereabouts in an era without cell phones, but they definitely could and did.)

"I'm sorry," I told Steve, "I'm in Minnesota for a two-day trial."

"Well, we'd like you to get on a red-eye plane right now to bring you to Oakland," he said.

"I'm sorry, I can't do that. I gave Minnesota my word."

"Okay, but just so you know, we'd like to have you here," he assured.

The next day at practice, Vikings personnel gave me workout clothes, but I didn't even practice. The coaches didn't even say anything to me.

The second day was also uneventful. I caught a few punts and did a little footwork, but that was it. *What was going on?*

The following day, Minnesota had a team meeting heading into their first regular-season game, and the Vikings head coach, Bud Grant, acknowledged my presence for the first time…the first time in two days.

"Randy," he said, "stand up and give us a scouting report."

Guess who they were playing that week.

The Denver Broncos.

I was *livid*. They didn't want to bring me in for a two-day trial. They just wanted to tap into the Broncos playbook. I lost all respect for Bud Grant.

"Coach, I've heard what your strategy is," I said vaguely, "and you seem to understand the speed of Rick Upchurch and the skill of Craig Morton. Seems like you guys have everything under control."

And then I sat back down.

I remember looking over at Jeff Siemon, a longtime friend who had actually played at Bakersfield High. He just shook his head in disgust. He could tell what was happening and immediately understood why they had brought me in.

I was very frustrated—especially considering that I had declined a two-day trial with Oakland to uphold my agreement with the Vikings. But I was beginning to catch onto the business side of things.

So I got on the phone with Oakland as soon as I could. I hopped on the next plane, and they ended up adding me to the roster.

Having gone to the Super Bowl the year before with the Broncos, being on the Oakland Raiders felt as if I had stepped over to the dark side, like I was in the enemy's camp. It was a strange culture. You would walk into meeting rooms, and there would be players smoking cigarettes. Very odd. John Madden was a great coach who had the respect of every player in the locker room, but it was just a different vibe in Oakland—one that I wasn't used to.

Toward the end of my second week on the Raiders' roster, I saw Steve Ortmayer in the locker room and approached him.

"Steve," I said, "I just got married—"

"You did?" he interrupted. "You need to bring her out, Randy. She needs to be here with you."

I talked to my wife and suggested that she leave Monday and drive twelve hours from Albuquerque to Bakersfield, stay for a night at my parents' house, and then complete the four-hour trip to Oakland on Tuesday.

Against the Packers, I was given an opportunity to return a kick, but unfortunately it was deep in the end zone, so I had to take a touchback.

Interestingly, the next morning, our day off, I received a call from Red Miller, the head coach for the Broncos. When I heard him on the other end, I was shocked and confused. It wasn't customary for an opposing coach to call a player on another team's roster.

"Randy, I'm not supposed to be calling you right now," Coach Miller said, "but I just want you to know that Oakland put you on waivers this morning. If you clear waivers, we want you back here."

My heart sank. I hadn't heard that I had been released. "Coach, is there a spot on the roster for me?" I asked.

After all, the Broncos were the ones who had released me to begin with.

"Well, you'll be on the hideout team," he replied. "Just like before, Randy. You know that once I can put you on the roster, I will."

I knew that Coach Miller was a man of his word, but I wanted to still consider other possibilities since my goal was to be on an active roster.

After the conversation, I immediately called my wife and told her not to drive to Oakland. Luckily she hadn't left yet or else I would have had no way of reaching her. The funny thing is that I always told her, "If you marry me, I'll show you the world." She was driving all around the country as I hopped around from team to team in the NFL.

Strangely, the entire day went by, and no one from Oakland called me to inform me that they had placed me on waivers. Weird.

The next day at the facility before practice, I killed time mulling around the locker room before getting dressed. I was embarrassed and wanted my teammates to make their way toward the practice field before I confronted one of my coaches. Once the locker room emptied out, I walked up to Steve Ortmayer and said to him, "Steve, does someone need to talk to me about something?"

"Yeah," he said awkwardly, "one second." And then he disappeared only to return a couple minutes later to say, "Mr. Davis (yes, *the* legendary Al Davis, owner and general manager of the Oakland Raiders) is sending his car over. Bring your playbook."

I understood immediately what the Raiders were trying to do: *They were trying to get an extra day of practice out of me for free.* Man, that ticked me off. The NFL, more than anything, is a business.

My meeting with Al Davis was bizarre, to say the least. I entered his office, sat down, and was slightly nervous. It was intimidating sitting there on the other side of his desk. Mr. Davis sat across from me with his big, goofy glasses, looked at me with his hands folded, and started bombarding me with questions.

"Randy, what do you think of Fred Biletnikoff?" he asked.

"What do you mean?" I responded.

"As a receiver, what do you think of him?"

"Mr. Davis, he's been a great receiver. But he's not as fast anymore, and he's easier to cover."

"What do you think of Mark van Eeghen?" he prodded, asking me about our full-back.

"Mr. Davis, that guy is hard to tackle. He's good. Really good. Bruiser of a running back."

"What do you think of Cliff Branch?" (Cliff was another one of our wide receivers.)

I thought the questions were odd, but all I could do was answer him.

"A world-class receiver. One of the best." Then I said, "Mr. Davis, why are you asking me these questions?"

"Oh, I'm interested in what other players think of the people on our team," he said matter-of-factly. "We brought you in to see if you would fit, and you do, but as you know, we don't need eight defensive backs. So we are going to release you, but we'd like you to be available when we need you."

Then the Raiders got me the first flight they could back to Bakersfield.

I WAS UNAWARE of how I was placing my self-worth in my performance as a football player. Whereas last chapter it was my search for affection through romantic relationships that was beginning to spiral out of control, this time it was my search for approval through football. So much of my identity was tied to my dream of playing in the NFL that when that dream began to fade, my identity consequently began to crumble. In many ways, I had an identity crisis.

Each of us has something in our lives that tries to rob us of our identities. I had falsely elevated football, and the struggles in that realm mentally and emotionally tortured me.

I felt as if I was being tossed around by the world, hopping around from place to place, getting cut by team after team. I was frustrated and discouraged. I just didn't seem to fit anywhere. Ever feel that way?

After a great season the year before—making the Detroit Lions regular season roster and the Denver Broncos playoff roster—it felt like I was once again on the outside looking in. It had become very clear to me that there was no regard for individuals when it came to professional football.

This was also the first time in my life that I had the feeling that I was failing in football. In high school, I was considered by others to be a star player. In college, I was considered by others to be a star player. In the NFL, I felt like an afterthought. And when my performance fell short of expectations, it left me scrambling.

As frustrated as I was, the reality was that it was *amazing* how far I had made it in the NFL. A kid from little Oildale who was told that he was too small and too slow to play college football now playing in the NFL—think about that! The truth is that our lives are miracles, but our struggles—and how we tend to focus on the negative aspects of our lives—often seem to blind us

> *"The truth is that our lives are miracles, but our struggles—and how we tend to focus on the negative aspects of our lives—often seem to blind us from this reality. There were blessings all around me but I didn't even acknowledge them because I was tunnel visioned."*

from this reality. There were blessings all around me but I didn't even acknowledge them because I was tunnel visioned.

My expectations were just so darn high. And my expectations were high because my identity was tied to what I did. What I thought of myself was tied to my success or failure in football.

I had heard throughout my faith walk—from the very beginning—that the things of this world can't fulfill you, but now the rubber was meeting the road. It seems the world's ploys disguise themselves as being "the thing"—the be-all and end-all that is to be attained—when in reality the most important thing is to have a strong relationship with Christ.

At the time, however, I believed that attaining success in football would satisfy me. And because I was placing my identity in a game, I found myself at my wit's end. My experience in the NFL was beginning to feel like a broken record. Unfortunately, I was dreaming of *becoming* someone, not dreaming because I already *was* someone. There I was again, looking for something to convince me of my "enough-ness."

It's vital that we learn to find our worth in Christ. It's not about what people think about you; it's about what God says about you. In the world we live in, with the glamour and glitz, we are deceived into following what we think is the ideal lifestyle or perfect life, thinking *If I just get to this place…* or *If I just reach this goal…* or *If I just find my spouse…*, then I'll be happy. But it doesn't work that way. Joy does not come from the outside; it comes from within. It doesn't come from what we have done; it comes from what God has done.

But because of the internal spiritual truths that I had neglected, I found myself to be very unhappy. My dream of playing in the NFL seemed to be slipping away.

Identity Thieves

- Describe yourself. What do you think is the most important detail about you? Is it related to this world (for example, what you do for a living or what you've accomplished), or does it go deeper?

- What in this world tempts to define you? How does it tempt you? When are you most vulnerable to its temptations? Become aware of the world's ploys and your own weaknesses and triggers.

- How can you become more aware of who you already are? Who are you? Define yourself.

- Read John 17:20–26. What does Jesus say about our identities as children of God? How can this reality of divine union free us from placing our identities in what we do?

CHAPTER 11

From a Dorm Room
to a Living Room

I knew one thing: I couldn't keep hopping around the league, always asking my wife to drive to a new city. This wasn't the lifestyle I had envisioned when I sought to pursue my dream of playing in the NFL. I was exhausted. Frustrated. Longing for something more secure and consistent.

The year before, I'd spent time in two organizations: the Lions and the Broncos. That was manageable. But the following year, 1978, I had already been in three cities and with two organizations—all before the midpoint of the NFL season! It wasn't healthy for me. And it certainly wasn't healthy for my marriage.

Upon returning to Bakersfield to be with my wife after the debacle with the Oakland Raiders, I immediately received a call from the Los Angeles Rams, inviting me to a two-day trial. It seemed like a better opportunity than playing on the Broncos' hideout team, so I decided to pursue it.

I went to Los Angeles and had a *great* trial, probably the best tryout I had ever had. The coaches were impressed and told me that they were probably going to put me on the roster for next Sunday's game. Things looked promising.

But at the same time, I was also aware that I had been down this road before. I was hoping for my hard work to lead to fruition.

After the tryout, I was instructed to return to Bakersfield. As I was waiting at my parents' place for the Rams to give me some clarity, I received another call, this time from Peter Hadhazy, the general manager for the Cleveland Browns.

"We'd like to bring you in for a two-day trial," he said.

I paused and then bluntly said to him, "I don't think so."

Never had I said something like this to a general manager or head coach in the NFL before. I just felt like I didn't have anything to lose. As I mentioned, I was tired of the cycle.

"Why not?" Mr. Hadhazy questioned, surprised.

"I'm going to be honest with you…" I was ready to leave everything on the line.

I shared with him the story about what had happened to me the last three to four weeks.

Before hanging up, Mr. Hadhazy told me, "Take a little bit of time to think about this, and I'll get back to you."

Something about the conversation, and my desperate tone with a general manager in the NFL no less, gave me the feeling that perhaps this was the end of the road for me. *Even if the Rams do sign me,* I thought, *who's to say it wouldn't be the same thing all over again?*

"We need to pray and ask God if this is it for me—if I am done with football," I remember saying to my wife.

We prayed together and surrendered my future as a football player to the Lord, there in the den of my parents' home in Oildale. Looking back, it was an interesting place to pray such a prayer. So many of my insecurities that I had hidden throughout my life—and that were still hidden at this phase in my life—had spawned from my childhood in that place. But football had always given me an outlet—yes, perhaps to hide those insecurities with my performance on the field, but most importantly to express myself in a positive way and to unleash my anger through healthy competition. And here we were, praying in a place where both my future in football and my deep insecurities seemed to collide.

Shortly after our prayer, I received another call from Peter Hadhazy.

"Randy, I wanted to call you to put your mind at ease," he told me. "If we bring you back here and if you pass your physical, we are going to guarantee you a contract for the rest of the year, and we'll pay for your wife's expenses to come out to Cleveland. We will also pay for your living quarters because we know that we are bringing you in mid season."

I asked him, "Are you sure?"

"Absolutely sure," he confirmed.

So I got on a plane.

I passed my physical and was welcomed onto the Cleveland Browns. The Browns paid me more money than any other team had offered me. I was very pleased and thankful. My salary, interestingly, was one fifth of today's minimum.

My first day in Cleveland, I ran into former Dallas Cowboys running back and Super Bowl VI champion Calvin Hill (the father of NBA great Grant Hill) at the hotel that happened to be our living quarters. (Calvin had just been traded to the Browns.)

"Would you be interested in attending a Bible study tonight?" he asked.

I told him that I would really enjoy something like that. So that evening, I hopped in Calvin Hill's car, and he drove us to a Bible study that was held at a teammate's house.

When we arrived, we stood on the front porch and knocked on the door. We were greeted by none other than Don Cockroft.

Remember Don Cockroft? He was the Cleveland Browns punter-kicker who had spoken at the FCA camp I'd attended my senior year in high school and the guy who had inspired me to make a decision for Christ.

I couldn't believe it.

He welcomed us into his home, and we took a seat in his living room alongside fifteen of our Browns teammates. When the Bible study began, Don, who was leading the study, asked me what my name was and then said, "Since no one here knows you, how about you share your testimony with us?"

I looked at him, smiled, and said, "Absolutely."

Sitting alongside a number of my teammates like Dick Ambrose, Johnny Evans, Mark Miller, Gerald Irons, and a few others, I shared with them a little bit about my upbringing and the loss of several of my close friends in high school. And then I told them about the FCA camp that I was invited to attend my senior year of high school. I shared with them how the only reason I went to the camp was because of the chance to meet NFL players. And then I told them about Don Cockroft and the message he shared with the campers—how it resonated with me, penetrated my heart, and spoke truth into my broken life.

Everyone's eyes in the living room were glued on me and Don.

Isn't God unbelievable? How cool was it that He would allow me to team up with the guy who had led me to Himself? That's a special touch from God—and those special touches are all around us. Some are obvious; others you have to pay close attention to or you'll miss them.

Eventually, Don spoke up.

"I *have* to say something about that story," he reflected. "I remember that year, and the truth is that I was not going to go to the FCA camp that year because I felt like I was in a backslidden phase in my faith. I didn't feel *worthy* to go because of some of my personal struggles in my life and faith. But I'm glad that I went."

> "That's a special touch from God—and those special touches are all around us. Some are obvious; others you have to pay close attention to or you'll miss them."

We all agreed that night that it was not about what we say or do; it's about what God has said and done. We decided that if we ever had an opportunity to share our faith, then we would do it. We alone might not be worthy, but Christ makes us worthy. So we decided that night that we would cling to our worthiness in Christ whenever we did not feel qualified.

I WAS UNAWARE that I was yet to find my worthiness in Christ. It all made sense in theory, and I actively participated in the conversation at Don Cockroft's house that night, but truth be told, I was finding my worth in other things.

By this point, my Capitalistic Christianity was rampant in my spirituality. I wore my Christianity like a nice suit. It made me look good. In some senses, my Christianity was another way for me to receive affection and approval from others, as messed-up as that might sound. Having been a Christian for a while, I could quote Bible verses and offer insight, and I enjoyed being viewed as knowledgeable. I thought that I had all the answers. A self-righteousness was beginning to grow within me. I was becoming judgmental, looking down on others who didn't profess Christ or who lived differently than I did. A very black-or-white approach to life was beginning to unfold. I was becoming more and more rigid, something that would be taken to the next level once I had children. Once more, even in a faith-context, my identity was in what I did, not in who I was.

I didn't know it at the time, but this idea of Christ making us worthy—of God actually *loving* us and *liking* us and *accepting* us as we are—would be the most difficult thing in my life for me to grasp. The conversation my teammates had that evening at Don Cockroft's house would be one that I would return to decades later, one that I would struggle to truly understand.

It is perhaps the most difficult thing in this life to believe: that we are loved and accepted by God without having to do anything to earn it.

Grace is a mystery.

> "I didn't know it at the time, but this idea of Christ making us worthy—of God actually loving us and liking us and accepting us as we are—would be the most difficult thing in my life for me to grasp."

Mercy and Grace

- Do you believe that God loves you? Why or why not?

- Is there something in your past that makes you think that God might not love you? What is it?

- Is there a current struggle in your life that makes you think that God might not love you? What is it?

- In our performance-based, capitalistic society, why is something like mercy (not getting what we deserve) and grace (receiving something we do not deserve) so difficult to grasp?

- Read 2 Corinthians 12:8–9. How are flaws and weaknesses a part of the Christian life?

CHAPTER 12

The Crux of the Insecurity

The Cleveland Browns were great to me.

I spent the entire year with them, playing for new head coach Sam Rutigliano, who had been hired after Forrest Gregg had been fired the year before. To my surprise, unlike any of my other experiences with NFL organizations, the Browns did *exactly* what they said they were going to do from the outset. Exactly what Peter Hadhazy had told me on the phone. They were people of their word. And yes, I was able to have my wife by my side. I felt very blessed and very thankful to be in Cleveland.

I never started for the Browns that season, but I played in nine games, mostly on special teams on coverage and as one of the Browns' kick returners. On defense I was a backup in the secondary and even recovered a fumble in one game. Interestingly, by that point in my NFL career, I had played behind an All-Pro defensive back at each NFL organization I was with.

Denver: Louis Wright.

Detroit: Charlie West.

Oakland: Jack Tatum.

Cleveland: Thom Darden.

Overall, the 1978 season was a step in the right direction for the Browns organization. We finished with a .500 record (8–8) in the NFL's first year of expanding to a sixteen-game season, and at times we looked like a playoff team.

In the offseason, my wife and I returned to Albuquerque.

I hoped that I could continue playing with the Browns, but I had my doubts when they selected defensive backs in two of the early rounds of the NFL Draft. Still, the coaches brought me back for training camp, and I was given a shot at making the team.

Everything went well throughout training camp and the preseason. I was playing the best football I had ever played, and I felt that this, combined with what the coaches already knew about me and my work ethic, would work in my favor.

By the third preseason game, our starting strong safety, Tony Peters, who had entered training camp with an unnegotiated contract, was traded to the Redskins for a player who lined up at an entirely different position. I knew this was good news for me.

Turns out, I made the team and spent another season with the Cleveland Browns.

Instead of playing cornerback in 1979, though, I was listed as a safety on the depth chart, backing up strong safety Clarence Scott and free safety Thom Darden. Being the only white guy playing in the backfield, Thom hilariously used to call our group of defensive backs "Randy Rich and the Defensive Blacks." On a similar note, this was actually the first year that the Cleveland Browns had a white guy—me—and a black guy—Mickey Sims—room together on the road. I didn't think anything of it, and neither did he. But to some it was a big deal.

Throughout the year, I returned fewer punts and kicks but continued to play various roles on the special teams unit. Though I was not a starter, I felt like I was trusted and relied upon by my coaches. They knew that I would do whatever they needed me to do.

The 1979 season was again another step in the right direction for the Browns organization. We started the season 4–0, the best start for the Browns since 1963, which included a stunning 26–7 victory over the heavily favored Dallas Cowboys on Monday Night Football.

Ten games into the season, we sat at 7–3 with a chance of making the playoffs for the first time in seven years. Being in the AFC Central with the powerhouse Pittsburgh Steelers, who had won three of the last five Super Bowls, made it especially difficult to win the division, but we felt that we had a chance at winning the AFC Wild Card. We were on a roll. I think we played in three overtime games that year and won two of them. This was the start of people calling the team the "Kardiac Kids."

The buzz in Cleveland that season was electric. The energy was infectious. Many of us on the team lived in the same apartment complex, and it wasn't uncommon to return from a road trip to see the complex hallways and our doorways decorated with Browns colors and memorabilia. Sometimes we would find gifts outside our doors and not know who they were from. The congeniality of the Browns fans that season made us all feel really special. They were appreciative but not imposing. Passion flowed from that city like a river. And it was head coach Sam Rutigliano and the culture he implemented with the Browns that seemed to ignite the flames of the fan base.

With the Browns being one of the oldest franchises in the NFL, they have always had passionate fans. I can understand, years later, why it devastated the community when owner Art Modell attempted to relocate the Browns to Baltimore in 1995. The Browns belonged nowhere but Cleveland.

Unfortunately, as special as most of the 1979 season was, we lost the last four out of six games to finish with a 9–7 record and miss the playoffs.

Another season ended.

As for my personal life, my first couple years of married life were interesting. Honestly, our marriage didn't have the happiest of starts. No, it wasn't violent like my parents' relationship. But living together was stale and uneventful—stagnant—even though I was playing in the NFL, living a life that I had always dreamt about. Although we were living this lifestyle that *appeared* to be glamorous, there was a lot beneath the surface that was unsatisfying.

Being on the fringes of the Browns depth chart, I know that my stress often poured out into the relationship. I was edgy and angry a lot of the time, often aggravated that I wasn't playing as much as I wanted to. My approach to football began to take a toll on our marriage.

When you place your identity in something that is as unsteady and fickle as a career, it leads to emotional distress. Once again, I kept putting my identity in what I did, rather than understanding and believing that my identity was in Christ. I had also forsaken the glue and core of our marriage—Christ. Everything gets muddled when you place too much importance in the world.

After a bad day at practice, I sometimes took the brunt of my frustrations out on my poor wife. As I've heard it said, you take out your frustrations on the one you love. Again, this was the result of my inability to recognize my deeper insecurities. When excelling in your career is your everything, it's easy to leave the ones you love by the wayside and forget about their needs and feelings because you are so absorbed in yourself.

In the offseason, my wife and I once again returned to Albuquerque until it was time for me to report to training camp. Today, most players live in the city where they play, but back then, most didn't; players and their families would return to where they lived during college or their hometown in the offseason.

Unsure of my future in Cleveland, I had my wife remain in Albuquerque until preseason was complete and final cuts were made.

I made the final roster once again. My third straight season with the Cleveland Browns.

I remember feeling stoked and motivated as I geared up for another season. Here I was, one of seven defensive backs on the roster of a team in the National Football League. And not just any team, but a team that was really building something special. Many believed that this was the year we would go to the playoffs and perhaps even challenge the Steelers for the division title. We were still coached by Sam Rutigliano, who had been named the NFL Coach of the Year the previous season. And our defensive coordinator was the newly acquired Marty Schottenheimer.

After the final cut when I was sure that I was on the team, I told my wife that she could come out to Cleveland for the season. My parents decided they would drive her out so that they could catch a game—their first game since the preseason game years earlier when I'd been unexpectedly cut by the Broncos. So the three of them began the long, thirty-hour drive to northern Ohio.

Heading into the week of practice before our first game of the regular season against the New England Patriots, I remember noticing that my roles on the special teams depth chart had been diminished. I didn't really think much of it at the time because at the defensive team meeting, Coach Schottenheimer had called my name several times as he explained the roles for the week. The thought crossed my mind: *Maybe they are going to use me more on defense this year instead of on special teams.* Looking back, I can see that I was fooling myself: I was there for one reason only, and that was to be a special teams player.

After our meeting, I was walking down the hall of the facility when Cleveland's director of player personnel asked me step into a side office.

"Randy, I hate to tell you this," he said, "but Coach Sam needs to talk to you and said to bring your playbook."

Those famous words.

I was stunned.

What was going on?

Coach Schottenheimer had just told me moments before what my role was for the week heading into our game on Sunday. And now I was getting asked to meet with my head coach and bring my playbook?

By the time I entered Coach Sam's office, walking past all my teammates dressed in their pads and headed the opposite direction toward the practice field, I had moved from shock to anger.

"Sam, what the heck is going on?" I said directly.

I have always respected Coach Sam, but in the heat of the moment, I was very upset. I was mad because my wife and mom and dad were somewhere between Albuquerque and Cleveland, and I had no way to get a hold of them to tell them to turn around. This same thing had happened years before in Denver. I was beginning to think that I should ask my parents not to come to my games.

Past feelings of embarrassment and humiliation returned.

"Randy," he consoled, "we've been working on a trade for Joe DeLamielleure, an All Pro offensive guard for the Bills, and we've decided to go with six defensive backs to make room for him."

"Sam, how long have you been working on this trade?"

"A couple weeks," he admitted.

"My mom, dad, and wife are somewhere between Albuquerque and Cleveland right now, driving out here. You could've told me you were working on a trade."

"We didn't want to tell you because if the trade didn't work out, then you would be on the team."

"Man, that just pisses me off," I said bluntly.

I would later thank Coach Sam for everything that he and the Browns organization did for me—and the opportunities they gave me—but in the moment, I was livid. Such is the nature of the NFL, however.

After getting cut, I then had go *back* down to the locker room, change *back* into my street clothes, and walk *back* out to the parking lot, where I could grab a shuttle *back* to the team hotel. And the only way to get back to the parking lot was to walk right through the practice field. I had seen others make the walk before, and my heart always grieved for them. Everyone sees you. Everyone knows what took place. I called it the "Walk of Shame."

I eventually made the lonely walk through the practice field and to the parking lot. A couple of my friends on the team saw me and threw their hands in the air, as if to say, "What the heck is going on? What are you doing?"

I shrugged and kept moving, eventually boarding the hotel shuttle.

When I got back to my room, I started gathering my stuff. The Browns had called me and said that they had a flight out for me later in the evening and that a car would be there to pick me up. Meanwhile, I was thinking, *Where are my parents and my wife?*

After practice was over, some of my close brothers in Christ returned to the hotel and prayed with me in my despondent state. They also prayed that my wife and I would be able to connect somehow over the phone. Our concern was that she and my parents were going to make the entire journey.

No more than a few minutes later, she called me at the hotel and told me that they had made it to St. Louis.

"Honey, turn around," I said. "I'll meet you all in Albuquerque."

"You've got to be kidding. You're teasing, right?" she asked, shocked.

"No, I just got released. I'll be in Albuquerque when you guys get there."

I wanted our conversation to be over. I was embarrassed and disappointed in front of my family again. I felt like I was back in my hotel room with my parents when I had gotten unexpectedly cut by the Denver Broncos. This seemed like another Groundhog Day. Same story. Different team. Different part of life.

I never played in the NFL again. Although I'd just made the Browns' roster for the third straight year, I also noticed around this time that my left shoulder, the one I had injured years before while tackling Walter Payton, was only getting worse and slowing me down. This was what was taking place on a practical level.

Three games away from securing my NFL pension—that's where my journey in football came to an end. I knew when I was released by the Browns that it would be difficult to fight my way back onto another NFL roster. A lot of marginal players back then were caught in that scenario and got blackballed when it came to receiving their pensions—a scenario that doesn't happen in today's game because of the changes that have been made in the NFL. Kind of like how a company might fire an employee within a year or two of receiving his or her retirement package. My bum shoulder didn't help matters.

Plus, after my career ended with the Browns so abruptly, the wind came out of my sails. I was invited by my old defensive backs coach for the Broncos, Bob Gamble, who was now the defensive backs coach for the Houston Oilers, to camp in Houston, and I made it through three preseason games, but even he could tell that I wasn't the same.

"What's wrong with you?" he asked me one day at practice. "You don't seem like you have the step you used to have."

"To be honest, Coach," I said, "I would just like to get my three games."

But they released me—and understandably so, I guess. I just knew it was over.

I hope, however, that this does not sound as if this is a sad ending to my journey in football. According to the NFL Players Association, the average length of a player's career is a little more than three years. That was the exact length of mine. I am so thankful for the organizations—especially the Denver Broncos and the Cleveland Browns—who took a chance on a small, white guy from Oildale, California, who was told that he was "too slow" and "too small" to play at a major university. Not only did I play for a big school in the Mountain West Conference, but I also held my own in the NFL and am happy to say that I made several NFL teams.

These days, I'm one of only a couple thousand players and head coaches who possesses a Super Bowl ring (runner-ups get rings, too) in the NFL's half-century existence. I did all that I could with the talents that had been given to me, tried to nourish and multiply those talents, and never allowed the labels that others put on me to determine my fate. I am happy to hang my hat on that. God was the one who opened and shut the door to the NFL, a platform that He allowed me to use later on in my journey.

I WAS UNAWARE at the time, however, that the biggest struggle in my life wouldn't come from others' opinions of me but rather my own opinion of myself.

"What would it take for me to believe that I was enough now that football was over? When would I really believe that what God says about His children is true—that we are loved, whole, and enough?"

I had proved to the doubters who labeled me in football that I was good enough to not only play at an NCAA Division I university but also in the NFL, but I was still wrestling with who I was. I was still dealing with my own self issues.

What would it take for me to believe that I was enough now that football was over?

When would I really believe that what God says about His children is true—that we are loved, whole, and enough?

Awakening to Wholeness

- What do you feel like you need to prove to yourself to attain self-worth? Why do you feel like you need to prove it?

- What do you feel like you need to prove to God? Why do you feel like you need to prove it?

- Could it be true that you are already loved by God as deeply as you could possibly be loved? Why or why not?

- Read Matthew 16:26. Discuss a time in your life when you were trying to "gain the world." What did this pursuit do to you internally?

PART II:
LIFE

What Do You Do When the Cheering Stops?

CHAPTER 13
The Biggest Mistake of My Life

If your identity is in what you do instead of who you are, left to yourself, you're nothing but a mess.

An article in *The Washington Post* in 2006 said that 78 percent of NFL players are divorced, bankrupt, or unemployed within two years of leaving the game because of the deep emotional and psychological issues that remain. When a player is forced to retire or walk away from a sport that he has played since his youth and when he no longer receives the praise and elevation he enjoyed at each level of the game, it leaves a gaping hole in his psyche. It can be earth-shattering when a player suddenly loses the status, name recognition, income, and perks of being a professional athlete.

Although I was not divorced or bankrupt or unemployed within two years of leaving the NFL, there was still a void in me. When you place your identity in something for a long time, it is inevitable that there will be a gap when that thing is gone. I think this is true for anyone who has done or been committed to something for a long period of time and suddenly loses that thing.

When my first autumn without football came around, I found myself getting an itch to do something, and I couldn't figure out why the angst was so heavy. It was difficult for me to watch football on television my first couple of seasons out of the league. I saw my friends still playing and felt that I could still be playing at that level. I sometimes couldn't help but ponder the question, "How long could my career have gone had I been given the opportunity?" After all, each year I'd had a brand new defensive backs coach who I'd had to prove myself to. The general feeling every time I reported to training camp was that I had a new coach who was looking at me and thinking, "What's this short, white guy doing here?"

But now the only question was this: *What's next for me?*

I had obtained a degree with an emphasis on biology from UNM, but I had no idea what to do with it. I could teach high school biology classes or coach football, but I didn't really want to do either of those.

After my wife and I moved back to Albuquerque, a place that we dearly loved, I applied for several jobs: an assistant athletic director position at a university, a public relations position at a bank, and a development officer at a nonprofit radio station called KLYT, the oldest contemporary Christian music station in the United States. The first two jobs fell through, but I was offered the job at KLYT, so I figured that I ought to accept unless I wanted to be a part of those daunting NFL financial statistics.

I worked there for a year and a half, barely making ends meet. We had no health insurance or benefits. On top of that, my wife and I also had a baby—our first of three daughters—while I was there.

At around that time, another radio station in town, an AM for-profit Christian radio station called KKIM, offered me a sales position that included a salary, insurance, and a commission plan. There, thanks to KKIM's general manager Doug Martin, who is a dear friend of mine to this day, I began to understand and learn the mechanics of operating a radio station. I loved the people and seemed to be good at sales—Doug told me that I had a convincing way of getting clients to purchase airtime with the station.

A year or so after I was hired, I was promoted to sales manager, and a year or so after being promoted to sales manager, Doug was moved to a station in Tucson, Arizona, and I was promoted to the general manager of the station.

The way I managed KKIM seemed to mirror the way I approached football, spirituality, parenting, and, well, just about everything in my life. Much of my life at this point seemed to flow from the grace-lacking paradigm of Capitalistic Christianity—performance, performance, performance. I demanded excellence and wanted results. I wasn't a tyrant, but I might as well have been a dictator.

Looking back, I'd imagine that I wasn't the most-liked boss my employees ever had. I was feared. And if my demands weren't met, I would use anger to control the situation—that same old story again. I'm sure that I was difficult to get along with. I had high expectations, and if someone wasn't there to "play ball," so to speak, I was hard on that person.

I was an unhappy and angry person at home, too. Anger, once more, reined. I was not a kind husband, and my attitude created a rift in my marriage. Why I was so angry, at work and at home, I'm not entirely sure—I guess I just expected things to be better; I thought I'd be happier. In my performance-based mindset, I had constructed a false-reality: one that was defined by high, unrealistic expectations that were impossible for others to meet. And instead of working on myself or my attitude, I lashed out. I was far from a kind husband, and though we only had one child at the time, I would go on to become a mean father, too.

I would say that the underlying issue in my marriage was this: I didn't have an introspective bone in my body. I had buried all of my issues and was simply reacting to them through anger whenever something didn't go my way—like an immature child. And this repression was having a very negative effect on my marriage.

Why wasn't I introspective? I guess I just thought that I was always right. In my world, it was my way or the highway. I barked orders. I hardly listened. And because I wasn't open, it was impossible for me to confront my marital issues. I was blind to them because I chose not to see. Sadly, I was merely continuing the cycle of abuse that I had witnessed in my father—someone who often lashed out in anger and ran around behind my mom's back. I might have *thought* that I was living differently than him because of my Christian faith—because I worked in ministry—but my Christianity was continuing to become more and more of a facade.

I knew that there were serious problems in my marriage, but I was ashamed to attempt to name them or bring them to the surface. Here I was, leading a Christian radio station—what would it look like if I had to go to counseling with my wife? In the '70s and '80s there was the perception in faith communities that if you went to see a counselor, you were somehow missing the mark. There was a false expectation from within the church that if you were a Christian and the Holy Spirit was leading your life, then you shouldn't have serious problems. And if you *did* have serious problems, then it was assumed they were because you weren't letting the Holy Spirit lead your life. These perceptions only fueled my performance-driven approach to faith. If I had problems—and I did—then I thought they must've existed because I wasn't working hard enough.

Anyway, I suppressed it all.

This is the most difficult section in this entire book to write.

I wish I did not have to include it, but I feel like it would be dishonest for me *not* to include this part. For the sake of transparency....

It's sad what your mind can do when you suppress what you know you need to deal with. I knew that things were not right in our marriage. But I didn't deal with it. My love language is physical touch, but there were real intimacy problems between me and my wife. I did not feel like I was good enough, and I once again found myself on a reckless search for affection—and this time it reached a level of desperation.

There's that cycle again: rejection, anger, sin. How could I have been so stupid as to think that those issues didn't need to be discussed or dealt with? Deep down I knew I needed someone from the outside to come in and shine some light on our problems, but I wasn't willing to get outside help.

All of this led to an implosion, the biggest mistake in my life.

Over the course of several months, I betrayed my wedding vows and cheated on my wife.

And, sadly, I even justified it in my mind. I told myself that going out with somebody else would take the physical pressure off my wife. It's crazy how you can justify something that you know is wrong. For years, I had suppressed my insecurities and had gone through life reacting to the things I didn't understand instead of taking the initiative to navigate through them.

I WAS UNAWARE of how my drastic decision-making was a result of my reckless, foolish approach to life; I had ventured through life ignorantly thinking that I didn't need to deal with what was underneath. Running to God—seeking both outside counsel and certainly the guidance of the Holy Spirit—would've required introspection and surrender. And not only had I neglected what was going on beneath the surface in my own life and in my marriage; I had also neglected some of the straightforward, practical teachings of the Bible regarding the Christian faith and marriage. My ego was running rampant, and I was apathetic toward the consequences.

Like King David, who notoriously slept with Bathsheba, the wife of Uriah, in 2 Samuel 11, I was searching for affection at all costs—which involved neglecting my faith and all that God had done for me in my life. Instead of taking every thought captive, as 2 Corinthians 10:5 instructs, I simply acted according to my ego and my cravings in the flesh.

> *"Every choice you make in this life is like throwing seed onto the ground: it will grow to become something one day."*

Though my wife and I tried to work out our problems and sift through my infidelities, these sins eventually returned to haunt me.

Every choice you make in this life is like throwing seed onto the ground: it will grow to become something one day. And the choices I made deeply wounded the relationships I cared about the most.

Beneath Our Sin

- Consider your biggest battle with sin in your own life right now. Where does the struggle come from? Is it related to an insecurity? How can you tackle the insecurity?

- Before you do something that you know is wrong, do you consider the potential consequences? Why or why not? Give an example of a time that you considered the consequences and a time that you didn't.

- Becoming aware of your sin isn't legalism. Rather, it allows you to become more fully alive by identifying where some of your reckless, unhealthy decisions come from so that you can live a healthier, more well-balanced life. What are some additional intentional steps you can take to become more fully alive?

- Read James 1:13–18. What does Scripture say about sin and desire? What desires are swarming within you right now? (Some desires are natural, but it is still vital to become aware of them so that these cravings do not lead to you hurting yourself or others.)

CHAPTER 14
Another Performance, Another Fig Leaf

A year or so after my infidelities became known to my wife, the board members at KLYT, the first radio station that I had worked for after my NFL career had ended, approached me and said that they wanted to take me out to lunch.

I had no idea what this meeting could possibly be about, but they explained to me at the restaurant that they were at a place, as a board, at which one of three things was going to happen with the station: They were going to: (1) sell it to a top radio format out of Reno; (2) shut it down; or (3) give it to me.

Before venturing too far down the road of the third option, I began to share with them some of the horrible decisions I had recently made in my marriage. Many of them, being Christian leaders in the Albuquerque area, were already aware of my actions. They acknowledged my confession and asked me what I had done to restore my relationship with my wife. After explaining to them the process I had gone through—which included counseling (albeit, looking back, it was not the sort of in-depth counseling I should have dedicated myself to)—they still seemed willing to pursue the option of turning their ministry over to me and a new board of directors.

I asked for some time to discuss the opportunity with my wife and to consider what this might mean to my current employer—who had worked with me both through the tragedy in my marriage and through the reconciliation and restoration process.

My wife and I discussed it and felt the Lord was leading me to transition to KLYT. Honestly, I was surprised that God would show me favor after the horrible mistakes I had made in my marriage.

We decided to give the opportunity at KLYT a shot.

As for my wife and I, we had tried to go to counseling after my infidelities, but counseling was difficult. Whenever I was confronted with something in therapy, I took it deeply personally. I cannot speak for my wife, but I can say that on my end, I was unwilling to humbly receive the counselor's advice and confront my own ghosts. I didn't want to acknowledge my problems.

You would think that something as serious as what I put her through would force me to deal with my deepest issues, but it did not. I was in denial. Like King David, my pride was so blinding that I failed to see my sin. And ironically, once the opportunity at the radio station presented itself, my focus began to shift from healing my marriage to building the radio station into a place of success. Instead of dealing with our pain, the easiest thing to do was to distract myself. My passion for ministry, in this sense, became a curse because it distracted me from reality. By the way, I know it might sound strange for me to talk about my passion for ministry amidst the serious failures in my own life, but that just goes to show you how much of a hypocrite I was—how dichotomous of a life I had constructed.

My wife and I remained together regardless. We had just had our third daughter (our oldest girl was four and a half, and our middle daughter was two and a half), and we didn't want them to grow up in a broken family. Plus, I didn't like the label of "divorce"—it wasn't good for the facade.

And so we settled into the unfortunate reality that was our marriage. We remained husband and wife, friends, and colleagues, but we didn't enjoy the love life you would expect in most marriages. My "Christian faith" even remained intact; I just didn't practice the introspection in our marriage that the Christian faith entails and requires.

So was it faith at all?

Transitioning into the opportunity at KLYT was, in many ways, scary on a personal level.

Not only had my wife and I just had our third daughter, but we had also just built a new home. Not to mention it was shocking when I finally settled in and got my hands on the station's financial books for the first time.

The station was only making $750 per month. Seriously.

And my skeleton budget was about $8,000 per month.

Upon acquiring the station, I quickly realized that I needed some cash to make it work. So I approached a business friend in the community who had a heart for ministry. He gave me three months of operating capital to get us up and running.

Within the next two years, we were generating forty thousand dollars a month. The growth was incredible to watch. We grabbed onto the coattails of the Holy Spirit and went for a ride that we never imagined.

And for the next nineteen years, our momentous ride continued.

Not only was KLYT the oldest contemporary Christian music station in the country, but thanks to our team and all the talented people who worked there, it became one of the leading radio stations in the country for Christian music. We won several state and national awards—things like "Station of the Year," "Broadcaster of the Year," and even "Sports Station of the Year." Not only were we using music as a tool to help others, but we were also using sports—two mediums deeply ingrained in today's culture.

The growth of our station led to Christian artists *wanting* to come to Albuquerque, of all places, because of the exposure we would give them. DC Talk, for example, booked their debut concert in Albuquerque because we could sell out auditoriums. Steven Curtis Chapman did his first live all-band concert in Albuquerque.

Across the state of New Mexico and into Colorado, we also developed over fifteen broadcast translators, which is basically a transmitter that repeats the signal of a station into a different area. Quite simply, we replicated KLYT in other communities by multiplying its signal. Because of KLYT's popularity in every corner of New Mexico, we took some bands on a three- or five-city tour throughout the state. I would travel with a lot of the artists, which was a blast. Sometimes I would fish with Steven Curtis Chapman or go hunting with Geoff Moore. It was an experience that I never believed I deserved. We were succeeding locally, statewide, and nationally as a premier Christian radio station.

Another program that we created at the station was a program called "Change Your World"—a school assemblies program where we provided a religiously neutral presentation to schools with a message that used biblical truth to teach integrity. The program was near and dear to my heart because of my childhood and the lack of direction I received from my parents. It was other people—like my brothers, Mr. Newbrough, Coach Eliades, and Coach Briggs—who had come alongside me and taught me fundamental principles that set me on the right path. I hoped to play a similar role for some of the children in the schools we were serving.

The idea for the program stemmed from a time when I was playing in the NFL and a football chaplain named Doc Eshleman—the father of Paul Eshleman (a key figure in producing *The Jesus Film*)—had the idea to assemble a group of NFL players in the offseason to give motivational talks to youth, messages that were religiously neutral but had biblical influence.

Doc told us that the three types of "most influential" people in America were athletes, actors, and performing artists. Being athletes, we could either use our platform to build up others or build up ourselves. I wanted to use my platform—my jersey—for the good of others, just as Don Cockroft had done for me when I'd heard his talk and asked Jesus to come into my life.

I was a part of Doc's program for several years while I was a player, and I hoped to impact others in that way—using my platform for the good of someone else.

Doc's program always stuck with me. While overseeing KLYT, I wanted to do something that had community impact, and developing a similar program to Doc's seemed to be a natural fit. "Change Your World" was another reason why KLYT was so recognized in the state and around the country—we were doing things that no one else was doing.

I was very involved in the program, traveling around and speaking at different schools in an effort to inspire youth to make good decisions. Oddly enough, as I write this, it seems strange that I would lecture others about integrity when, at one time, I didn't have integrity in my own marriage. Over the years, I had become accustomed to compartmentalizing things in my life.

During KLYT's rise, I sometimes thought to myself, "God, I can't believe that you would allow me to be a part of the blessing at KLYT." I knew that there were current board members and other ministry leaders in the community who knew of my failures, but I was grateful that they had shown the mercy that they had. There were others who distanced themselves from me, and I understood why, but they tolerated the fact that I was in the position because of the impact we were having on the airwaves.

I am sure that part of my motivation and drive in ministry was to somehow make up for the bad things that I had done. I now know that God doesn't keep score in that way, but deep within me at the time I felt that He kept score with me *specifically* because of the severity of my moral failures in my marriage. What I wasn't aware of was that I was keeping score; God wasn't.

During those two exciting professional decades, there was a mask over my personal life.

My family and I had moved into our dream home—a beautiful ranch-style home that, yes, sat at the end of a long driveway. Our three-acre property rested in the valley of the Rio Grande River and was surrounded by a white-pipe fence. We also had a barn, a tractor, horses, dogs, and sheep.

But it was all an act.

Hypocrisy.

The issues in my marriage were still there. I might have re-established her trust after betraying her and forsaking our marriage nearly two decades before, but I hadn't dared to truly—and humbly—sift through the ever-present pain.

We *did* go back to counseling fifteen years into our marriage, with a focus on some of the challenges and trauma that we had recently unearthed from my wife's childhood, but I was just as ignorant. One day I remember our counselor saying to me, "Randy, if the two of you do not deal with these issues, your marriage is going to fall apart."

"Why is that?" I remember foolishly asking. "I think we've worked through our problems."

My question and comment are reflective of what I ignorantly seemed to believe—that we had dealt with our problems just by being there in counseling. I can't speak for her, but I know that I never did the due diligence in humbly and introspectively sifting through the pain. That required hard, unenjoyable work.

My relationships with my daughters were just as bad. They were often the victims of unfair, harsh, and sometimes cruel discipline from me. I was hard on my girls—strict and legalistic. To be candid, I was verbally and emotionally abusive. And in their childhoods, I would often spank them out of anger. Sound like anyone? My techniques were a terrible way to parent, *especially* with daughters. I didn't realize it at the time, but in reflection I can see that I often used the tool of anger to gain control over my children and to frighten them into obedience. One of my daughters recently told me that growing up in our household often felt like they were trapped in a "living hell."

Because of everything I saw come across my desk at the station regarding the influences of the world and how it impacted young people's thinking and lives, I tried to establish some tall guardrails around my girls that were simply unfair and unproductive to the Christian life. Things were extremely regimented. I didn't let them listen to mainstream music, and I was very selective in the types of programs they watched on television. I was way too rigid. I lived with a black-and-white mindset in a gray world. I was dedicated to raising our children with more structure than how I'd been raised, but my desire to protect them combined with an irrational fear of anything "secular" sent me to another extreme—and I used fear and punishment as tools to manipulate them. I demanded excellence and perfection—unobtainable standards. Why was I so afraid of letting them make mistakes? Looking back, it amazes me that I was so judgmental toward my daughters when so much forgiveness had been extended to me from my wife, my friends, and the Lord.

I WAS UNAWARE at the time that I was using the "successes" at the radio station—the American Dream I had attained—to cover up everything that was beneath the surface in my personal life and in my household. You'd think that over time, the junk would have worked itself out, but the cycle simply repeated itself.

Instead of football being a facade, now it was ministry—and all the benefits that came along with our radio station's meteoric rise. I guess working in Christian ministry can do wonders in covering up your shame. It was the ultimate fig leaf, I suppose.

Overall, what's interesting to me about those nineteen years at KLYT is the realization that I was doing what I had always done. Just as I had covered my insecurities throughout high school and college and the NFL with my performance on the football field, I was covering my shame with my performance in ministry and my reputation in the community. My shame still existed, but I was covering it with my work. My anger in the household was out of control, but no one from the outside could have ever guessed that things were so dysfunctional.

> *"I did have the occasional fear: Could it be that at some point in time that God was going to knock on my door and ask me to bring Him my playbook?"*

I wrestled with shame—those hidden secrets that most didn't know about, the infidelities many years before, my anger and abusiveness with my daughters—but I was watching many great things happen at the station, and I felt good about that. I did have the occasional fear: *Could it be that at some point in time that God was going to knock on my door and ask me to bring Him my playbook?*

And so to prevent this, I did what I always did: I worked harder. I grappled to control all that I could. I ran the radio station and my family with an iron fist. I continued to construct the facade.

American Pharisees

- Do you use self-righteousness or spiritual actions to cover the insecurities or shame inside of you? Give an example.

- How are you using successes or elements of the American Dream to cover your insecurities? If you are a performer in this life, what is your stage?

- Think critically here: Does what you do outshine who you are? Is who you are contingent upon what you do? Discuss.

- Read John 4. What effect does the woman's shame have on her life? What was Jesus's response to her shame? How might meeting with Jesus transform your own experience with shame?

CHAPTER 15
A Morning with My Ghosts
in the Barn

While I was overseeing KLYT, one of the rules I put in place at the station was if for any reason a member were going through a divorce, he would need to relinquish his position and focus on restoring his marriage. Subconsciously, perhaps I wanted to put some guard rails in place to help prevent indiscretions that I was a part of many years before; or perhaps I was trying to hide my own ghosts with a mask of self-righteousness.

My overall attitude toward rules was much like that of the pharisees in the Bible. They seemed to dictate my entire attitude, at work and in my home with my wife and daughters. It's what is called the "Pharisaic Life": implementing rules and making harsh judgements in order to build up oneself. A lot of times, I judged people out of my own insecurities—I guess, to help me feel more secure. A foolish pursuit.

All of this was ultimately a byproduct of my performance driven-spirituality. It was Capitalistic Christianity exposed. I deceived myself into thinking that implementing strict rules would bring me, and others, closer to God. Rules were a way for me to control the spiritual process and for me to feel more righteous, like I had it all together. But that's nothing more than what the Pharisees did in Jesus's day. Their high, unobtainable standards were a way for them to build themselves up. It was always about keeping score. Perception. Self-righteousness. Maintaining control.

At the station, that's the way it was. I kept a tight, closed fist of control on the things we did at KLYT. In my mind, there was no room for error. Now I know that was a big fat lie. There's always room for error. God works through error. My friend, Dave Cauwels, once said to me, "Stay on your knees, Randy, so that when you fall, it's not very far." This posture, however, involves a life that is marked by humility. My life was far from that. I thought that I had it all figured out. I had used my rigid Christianity to build myself up.

After I made these rules at the station, there was one board member whose wife filed for divorce—for no apparent biblical reason—and he was asked to step down from his position. I know it hurt the man and certainly must have been confusing to him. Where was the grace that was extended to me?

I didn't realize it, but his life was the foreshadowing for what my life was about to become.

Heading into my twentieth year at the station, my father-in-law died.

And, one week after his death, my wife told me that she wanted me to move out, saying she needed a break. A few weeks after that, she began the process of filing for divorce.

Without going too deep into this out of respect for my ex-wife, I think there are several issues that led her to these decisions—most of which had to do with me, some of which had to do with her past. Her father dying was the event that pushed her over the edge, both practically and emotionally. It revealed what was already there—all the unresolved issues in play. All it took was a single incident to shatter the shell that I had constructed, to expose what I'd known was there all along but was too prideful to confront.

Doesn't it seem like the shell always seems to shatter? Doesn't the facade always seem to crumble?

The divorce had all kinds of fallout.

There was already a deep tension there between me and my daughters, stemming from my fear-based parenting and the harsh rules that I implemented—a tension that still exists to this day. And when my daughters found out about my infidelities, it was as if my hypocrisy was clearly revealed. Though my affairs had taken place many years before, to my daughters it felt as if they had just happened. Not to mention my daughters were sixteen, fourteen, and twelve—very formative years for them. I think that they had always felt that I was a hypocrite—seeing my life in ministry and hearing all the spiritual things I said but also simultaneously experiencing my rage and control in the household—but this revelation was the ultimate form of hypocrisy. How could I have been so strict and judgmental with them when I had made horrible mistakes in my life?

Second, it meant that I would lose my job, just like the man who had lost his job on the board. When the news surfaced that I was getting a divorce, there was a general feeling on the board at KLYT, which I agreed with, that "what's good for the goose is good for the gander." The rules applied to me, just as they had applied to that poor man a couple years before. As a generous display of kindness, the board gave me a severance package to help me heal and transition into the next phase of my life, but leaving a place that I felt like I had helped build was a difficult pill to swallow. I was not only losing my family at home; I was also losing my family at work.

As for the radio station, almost two decades of work seemed to crumble, which makes a person wonder: *Was it built by man or built by God?* Rumors abounded. Gossip unfolded. Many thought that my cheating was recent and had unfolded while I was at KLYT. Though this wasn't true, my sins had still been exposed. My ghosts had returned.

> *"Once more, I found myself projecting my own perception of myself onto God's view of me. How the world treats you based on what you do or don't do can sometimes make you think that's how God views you, too."*

Once more, I found myself projecting my own perception of myself onto God's view of me. How the world treats you based on what you do or don't do can sometimes make you think that's how God views you, too. I had always projected my performance-based identity in the football realm onto God—saying "These teams cut me or keep me based on my performance, so God must view me the same way"—and now I found myself doing the same in the realm of ministry. That dreaded day had arrived. It felt like the time had come for me to bring God my playbook. I was getting cut.

Following the separation, the best I could do was get out of bed. And I certainly didn't like going out into public. I was embarrassed. Ashamed. I had no idea what to do. I felt like my life was over.

I WAS UNAWARE of what God's grace actually was, what divine love actually meant. I'd never felt so unworthy in my life. Spiritually, I was destroyed.

Though I'd found meaning in my life working in ministry, I felt like I could never work in ministry again. I needed to find a job, and, despite the connections I had made in ministry over the years, I didn't reach out to any of them. I didn't dare. A couple of people who worked in the Christian world reached out to me, but I respectfully declined. How was I to continue working in ministry after the mistakes I had made?

I have not shared this with many people, but one day, after my wife and kids had moved out of our house, I woke up one morning and felt as if I was drowning in worthlessness and despair. I took a loaded .357 out into my barn and sat there for quite some time, contemplating why I shouldn't end my life right then and there. The enemy is always knocking on our door, seeking to steal, kill, and destroy. And, as crazy as it is, I asked myself that morning: *Does God view me the same way?*

> *"What was I worth now that the facade I had constructed to hide my insecurities had crumbled and left me exposed? What was I worth now that I had no control at all? What was I worth when the outlets I used to convince myself that I was enough were gone? What was I worth if all I had was God?"*

I sat there for about an hour—something that almost felt like an out-of-body experience—and was thinking some pretty crazy things. However, I felt like God was meeting me where I was. Suicide is such a selfish thing, and I realized I didn't want to add anything else to what I had already caused. But had I not had children, it's hard to say whether or not I would have done it. That's just how little self-worth I had and how much I hated what I had done to my loved ones.

What was I worth now that the facade I had constructed to hide my insecurities had crumbled and left me exposed? What was I worth now that I had no control at all? What was I worth when the outlets I used to convince myself that I was enough were gone? What was I worth if all I had was God?

Evaluating Self-Worth

- Talk about a time when your self-worth bottomed out. What led to this? Why did you feel the way you did?

- Talk about a time when you felt confident and close to God. What led to this? Why did you feel the way you did?

- What do you think God's opinion of you was when your self-worth was at its lowest low? What do you think God's opinion of you was at a time when you felt confident? What do you think God's opinion is of you now?

- If you think that God feels differently about you depending on your performance, what does this say about your perception of God?

- Read Romans 8:1–11. What does it say about condemnation? What does the cross of Christ tell us about God's reaction to sin?

CHAPTER 16
The Arrogance of Shame

It was as if everything I had always felt resurfaced: The desperate life I'd led in middle school and high school, searching for approval and affection through football and romance. The rejection I'd experienced in college and in the NFL. The underlying fear of not being enough.

The seeds of sin that were sown early in my life came back to haunt me.

As I mentioned earlier, every choice that is made in life is like seed planted in the ground. If it's good, you reap a good harvest. If it's bad, it might take a bulldozer to knock it down.

But this time, the shame and insecurity were even deeper because my worth was connected to my own personal failures *and* my spirituality—the deepest parts of who I was. In other words, at the core of my being, I felt like a failure. Before God, I felt like a failure. My sins had come back to haunt me. And I felt as if God was repaying me what I had deserved. Though I think I knew deep down that this wasn't true, it's how I felt. *Had I gone too far? How far was God willing to go to bring me back?* Just like when Jonah said to the sailors to throw him overboard during the storm so that their lives would be spared, I too felt like I was ready to be thrown overboard.

> *"Every choice that is made in life is like seed planted in the ground. If it's good, you reap a good harvest. If it's bad, it might take a bulldozer to knock it down."*

Throughout my life, whenever I heard about someone who had committed suicide or had attempted to commit suicide, I would sort of judgmentally conclude, "What would drive someone to do something so horrific?"

But suddenly I could see why someone might try to do such a thing.

Never did I think about suicide before that morning in the barn nor did I think about it after. But I could certainly understand how someone's self-worth could hit rock bottom, how they could conclude that life was no longer worth living. Never in my wildest dreams did I imagine that I could relate to such a sentiment, but all of a sudden, I could.

I felt like Job in the sense that I had lost everything—my family, my profession, and my reputation. But the difference between Job and me was that I was not the victim; I felt like I was the perpetrator. All of this was my fault. My life had collapsed beneath my feet, and I was the one who had constructed the floor.

For three months, I didn't do anything. I struggled to get out of bed. I was idle. Zombie-like in my existence. No purpose. No meaning. Three months might not sound like a long time, but for a doer and go-getter like me, this stagnancy reflected the depth of my despair.

Interestingly, one of my mentors from college, Jay, who I mentioned earlier, re-entered my life at around this time. He too had gone through a divorce and had fallen off the face of the earth when it came to ministry. I'm thankful he came back into my life when he did because I was able to relate to him on a different level: divorce in ministry. I felt like I had personally failed while trying to guide others in their relationships with Christ. It was interesting that someone who was one of my mentors in college and who had vanished because of his own divorce re-entered my life when he did. He helped to restore my spiritual well-being in the devastation of the divorce.

Another one of my good friends named Jim also met me in my depths. Sometimes I would get a call in the morning from Jay or Jim and they'd say, "Have you eaten breakfast today?" If I hadn't, one of them would insist on picking me up and taking me out to breakfast or to a coffee shop.

They made sure that I stayed healthy and took care of myself. They made sure that I got out of the house from time to time. I think that Jay especially understood how agonizing isolation can be when your self-worth is stripped, when you are plagued by shame.

Around this time, my friend Dois Rosser, the founder of International Cooperating Ministries (ICM) in Virginia, an organization that assists in church planting in indigenous communities around the world, reached out to me and offered me a job. Dois and I had met a little over a year before, and I had entertained the idea of going to work for him. He knew about everything that was going on with me in my personal life, but it did not stop him from pursuing me.

I politely declined his offer, however, believing that I was too damaged to return to ministry. There seemed to be an invisible line out there that said, "If you cross this, you're done"—and I felt like I had crossed it. I had accumulated too many failures, it seemed, for me to get back into doing what I really enjoyed. I wanted to work where I didn't feel as if I was being judged by my faith—which I understand is a crazy thing to think because no matter what we do, our faith should be on display. But it's how I felt.

While working at KKIM and KLYT all those years and helping those stations fundraise and partner with other organizations, it had been suggested to me that I'd do well in a field like insurance. Since I didn't feel like I could work in ministry ever again, I wanted to make a lot of money in an industry that would allow me to give to ministry.

In September, I began working for Manuel Lujan Agency, the largest independent insurance agency in the state of New Mexico. It was a family-owned agency directed by my friend, Larry Lujan. Larry and his brothers—Jerry, Joe, and Steve—really took me in and made me feel like I was a part of something. I worked there for over two years.

The Lujans were incredibly generous to me and kind. I feel that I will always be indebted to them because of the opportunities they gave me. It was difficult to transition from a ministry where the mission was to help people know Christ deeper to an industry that was certainly designed to help people but where the bottom line was always considered. The truth, however, is that we should have the attitude of ministry in everything that we do. But I had such a black-or-white, sacred-or-secular, dualistic approach to life that I didn't realize that I could have just as much of an impact on the world working in insurance that I could working in ministry.

I WAS UNAWARE that it wasn't God who was telling me that I couldn't get back into ministry—it was *me* telling myself that I didn't deserve to be in a position like that ever again. I just didn't feel like I had much to offer in terms of ministry.

In reflection, it seems to me that when we feel that we don't have much to offer, we must further explore where that lie that we are telling ourselves is coming from—because it's never from God.

But I didn't recognize that the things I was telling myself were lies. The truth is that we don't have a lot to offer God, but God doesn't view us that way. Whenever these self-deprecating feelings return today, it is as if I can hear God saying from the core of my spirit, "Randy, you have the gall, the arrogance, to say that what I created doesn't have any use?"

> *"When you are ultracritical of yourself and base your worth on your performance, you inevitably venture through life feeling discouraged and unworthy. You will always desperately search for something to convince you that what you really believe about yourself is not true. My lifelong search for affection and approval was really just a reflection of my inability to accept that I was loved by God."*

But at the time, I thought my inner dialogue was reality. And my internal dialogue as it related to my self-worth was toxic, because the foundation for my dialogue was based on my failures, my insecurities, and my incompleteness—not on the reality that God loved me in a way that was incomprehensible. I struggled to believe that I was full and that I was whole—not because of what I had done, but because of what God had done for me on the Cross and in my life. And the truth is that if there is a need for divine correction in our lives, it's because God loves us and wants the best for us.

When you are ultracritical of yourself and base your worth on your performance, you inevitably venture through life feeling discouraged and unworthy. You will always desperately search for something to convince you that what you really believe about yourself is not true. My lifelong search for affection and approval was really just a reflection of my inability to accept that I was loved by God. I had a warped mindset and had neglected the simple joys of Christianity.

Why did I make it so complicated? I guess I believed that I was a sinner at my core—not that I was loved. And by believing this, I unknowingly elevated my humanity and my works (my performance) above the mystery of grace.

It is perhaps the most arrogant thing that I could have done: to elevate my opinion of myself above God's opinion of me.

Your Perception vs. God's Perception

- Has there ever been a time in your life when you felt that you weren't doing what you were meant to be doing? Did you feel like you had a choice? Why or why not?

- Talk about a time when either your own perception of yourself or your perception of what God thought about you held you back. What's your perception of yourself now? What do you think God's perception is of you?

- What's the lens for your inner dialogue? Is it incompleteness or wholeness, your past failures or your future hope, your own critique of yourself and what you've done or God's affirmation of who you already are? Explain.

- Read John 21:15–19. How does Jesus reinstate Peter after his moral failures? How does Jesus give him worth once more? How does Jesus invite him back into purpose? In what areas of your life is God doing that for you?

CHAPTER 17
The Day that Liberty Cried

During those two years selling insurance, I was picking up my pieces and moving on from the divorce, but I was picking them up the same way I had always picked them up. The way I approached football. The way I approached ministry. The way I approached spirituality. By *doing* things and thinking that I could fix everything. I had certainly been humbled, but my dominant mindset was an actionable checklist:

- *What am I going to do?*
- *How am I going to do it?*
- *What's the game plan?*
- *How can I execute the game plan?*

Not that this was a bad mindset, but the reality is that I struggled to fully surrender my situation to God. I struggled to admit my helplessness. As I've mentioned before, I wanted someone to show me a playbook and not change the rules at halftime.

Jay was still speaking heavily into my life and helping me realize that I was more than my performance. But I was still a "human doing" and not a human *being*, as I've heard it said. If I wanted to get my life back in order, I felt like it was up to me to do so.

One time Jay challenged me with the question, "Why do you think that God created you?"

I thought about his question, one that I had never seriously considered. After giving the matter some thought, I responded, "To worship Him, to glorify Him, to honor Him, and to make myself available to Him."

Jay went on to explain to me that all the things I mentioned were a type of *doing*—actions that were up to me to complete. This "doing," Jay said, could be a byproduct of a life in Christ but not the reason why God created us. He then told me that we are made for fellowship with God, for *friendship* with God—by not doing anything at all.

"God didn't need a relationship with you; He *wants* a relationship with you," Jay told me. "God doesn't need us to do anything for Him; He *allows* us be a part of His work."

What Jay said to me made sense, but as a performance-driven person, the habits and thinking patterns of how I approached my faith were difficult to break. I liked how it sounded in theory, but I struggled to apply it. I needed to "let go and let God," as I've heard it said, but I struggled to do so. What did that even mean, anyway? I liked maintaining a sense of control. Surrender was far too scary.

> *"God didn't need a relationship with you; He wants a relationship with you. God doesn't need us to do anything for Him; He allows us be a part of His work."*

One reason I felt the need to pick myself up by my bootstraps and press on with my life had to do with discontentment in my heart. My relationships with my daughters were rocky. I felt alone and confused at church, as if I had disappointed my friends by getting a divorce. I was making a good living working at the Lujan Agency, but I still felt unsatisfied. My life was defined by regret. Had I not messed up, I would have still been doing the things that brought joy to my heart. Overall, I struggled to forgive myself.

Dois Rosser at International Cooperating Ministries (ICM) continued to check up on me during those two years. He always said to me, "You have a place here, Randy…whenever you are ready." But I still didn't feel like I could accept his generous job offer. I was in a sort of relational, spiritual, and professional limbo. And whereas I was repairing my relationships with my daughters and was perhaps opening myself up to new spiritual ideas, I didn't see myself ever being able to regain any sort of ministerial meaning and purpose, like I'd once felt I had.

During the summer of 2001, Dois called and asked me, "What are your thoughts about going to Cuba with us this September?"

I liked the idea and agreed to go. The invitation happened when very few Americans were able to visit the island.

Years before, back when I worked at KLYT, I had gone to Hyderabad, India, with Dois, and it was one of the most moving ministry experiences I ever had. It was inspiring to see how involved ICM was with planting and dedicating churches in the area, but it was also neat to see God at work while we were there. One day, after a long day of bus rides, my friend, David Cauwels (who had initially introduced me to Dois and the ministry of ICM), and I were walking down the streets of a crowded community in Hyderabad, when a little fifteen-year-old boy in his school uniform—a white polo shirt and navy blue shorts—approached us and asked us in his Indian accent, "Excuse me, what are you doing?"

We said that we were telling people about Jesus, and he responded, "I would like to know Jesus."

We had been taught, for safety purposes, not to share the gospel in the streets, so we invited our new friend Nagra back to the hotel to learn about Christianity. The next day, Nagra and a friend of his came to our hotel, and we continued our discussion. The church community there took Nagra under their wing, and we later heard that he went to a Bible college, paid for by David, and ended up working in full-time ministry there in India. Now Nagra is a pastor at an ICM church.

This kind of stuff seemed to happen all the time on these vision trips, and it was always a reminder to me of God's work in the world.

And it was for this reason, perhaps, that I agreed to go to Cuba with Dois—because I wanted to see God's hand at work again.

We flew to Cuba the first week of September with a small group of people, but during the trip, an unexpected tragedy unfolded.

A forty-year-old woman in our group named Bobbie—who was visiting Cuba because she wanted to see the churches that her family had sponsored but who had a terminal illness that we'd been unaware of—passed away on Saturday night in her sleep. On Sunday morning, Dois called for a team meeting at breakfast and said to us, "I have some good news and bad news. The good news is that Bobbie is with the Lord this morning. The bad news is that she won't be finishing the trip with us." We were stunned.

We ended up going to a worship service at a nearby church that morning, and it was moving to see how the Cuban people loved on us and helped to comfort Bobbie's father, who was also on the trip.

On Monday night at eleven o'clock, I returned home with a renewed perspective on life. Though Bobbie's death on our trip was shocking, we had all seen God work through that brokenness and through the love of the Cuban people. I went to bed, encouraged from the trip but absolutely exhausted.

The next morning, I woke up to a phone call from my middle daughter, who was a freshman in high school. "Dad," she said anxiously, "I'm scared. I think we're going to war."

"What?" I asked, confused.

"Turn on the television," she said.

I turned on my TV, and that's when I saw that the United States was under attack.

The September 11 terrorist attacks had fallen upon America. I had flown home from Cuba on September 10, 2001.

I sat there in my living room, utterly shocked as I watched the television.

My daughter came over to my house and sat there in my arms as we watched the second plane crash into the World Trade Center.

Later that evening, I prayed, "God, what the heck am I doing with my life?"

I WAS BEGINNING TO UNDERSTAND that it wasn't God who was holding me back; it was my mentality that was holding me back. There I was, building a career that didn't fulfill me, all because I couldn't forgive myself. I was in my own way.

Between Bobbie's unexpected death on our trip in Cuba and the terrorist attacks on September 11, I had realized how short and fragile life can be.

A week after the September 11 terrorist attacks, I gave Dois a call and said to him, "I'm ready to make a move. I can't move to Virginia. I need to live here to be close to my girls as I try to piece my family back together, but I would love to be a part of ICM if the offer is still available."

"You don't need to move here," he told me. "It'd be good to have an office out west, there in Albuquerque."

The time had come for me to take a step toward experiencing what made me feel most alive once more. This life was all that I had. It could end any moment. I could've been Bobbie on that mission trip. I could've been in one of the Twin Towers that tragically fell. Was I really going to let the stupid self-deprecating thoughts that I had—something that I *could* control—prevent me from fulfilling the plan God had for my life?

Shane & Shane, a Christian band, has a wonderful song called "Liberty." It resonated with me deeply at the time as I allowed God to rewrite my name, unshackle my shame, and open my eyes—as the lyrics say.

Submitting my resignation to the Lujan Agency was difficult because of all that they had done for me. They had provided a transition for me through one of the most difficult parts of my life. I didn't want to disappoint them, but I knew that I had to go. If I only had twenty-four hours in a day to do something, I wanted to spend it in ministry. It was how I was wired.

> *"Jesus had His arms open, inviting me into His presence, but my ankles were shackled with shame—and I was the one who held the key to the shackles! It was all in my mind."*

In reflection, I believe God kept inviting me back into something I was passionate about through Dois's pursuit of me to work at ICM, but I kept declining the invitation because of my own perception of myself.

I could identify with Peter, who messed up and denied Jesus three times, but instead of allowing Jesus to redeem my brokenness and welcome me back into purpose as Christ did with Peter (John 21:15–19), I wouldn't even allow Jesus to have a conversation with me because I didn't think that I was worthy of His time. Jesus had His arms open, inviting me into His presence, but my ankles were shackled with shame—and I was the one who held the key to the shackles! It was all in my mind.

In a sense, we become what we think. Our internal dialogue can consist of truth or lies, positivity or negativity. I didn't want to be shackled by the lies and negativity that flowed from arrogance any longer.

I'm not sure if I *really* forgave myself, but I knew one thing: it was time for me to be involved in ministry again. It was time for me, empowered by God, to begin to unlock the shackles.

Meaning and Purpose

- If you knew that you would die in five years, what would you do with your life now? What career would you pursue? Which of your relationships would you mend?

- Take responsibility of what you *can* control. In what ways are you in your own way?

- Do you feel disqualified from doing things that are associated with God or ministry or spirituality? Why or why not?

- Read Acts 9:1–19. What were the lengths to which God went in His pursuit of Paul? Consider the fact that Paul was a well-known persecutor and killer of Christians. What does this say about God's character that He would pursue someone with a wretched history like Paul's? How is God pursuing you right now? In what areas of your life do you need to accept God's pursuit of you and see more clearly?

CHAPTER 18
Wayne's Coat

One Sunday during the spring, I decided to attend a nearby house of worship called Hoffmantown Church. In the fallout of the divorce, a church community was something I craved and needed. What we need most in our lives is fellowship.

A Tennessean pastor named Wayne Barber, a giant of a man, had just become the head pastor at Hoffmantown, and I found myself immediately compelled by how he preached and what he preached about. On that first Sunday, I remember Wayne standing in front of the congregation and saying something along the lines of, "It's not about what you say or don't say, what you do or don't do; it's about what Christ has already done."

Wayne then proceeded to remove his sport coat and tell a story to the congregation: "The Christian life is a lot like what I am about to share with you," he began, holding his coat in one hand. "I'm a big man, and it's hard to shop for clothes. But when I went into the store and saw this coat hanging there, I thought, 'Boy, I sure hope that thing fits me.' So I put the coat on, and sure enough it fit perfectly. I bought it. And now this is *my* coat. I own it. And I'll prove to you that I own it...."

Wayne looked at his coat again, which he was still holding in his hands. "Since I own this coat, I can tell it what to do," he continued. "Coat, raise your right arm. C'mon, coat, don't let me down. Coat, raise your right arm. C'mon, coat, don't embarrass me in front of my friends.'"

Obviously, the coat did not raise its right arm.

"Folks," he continued, "this coat can't do anything on its own until I get in it. So I'll put it on and get inside it."

Wayne then lowered the coat and put his arms through its sleeves, once again wearing the jacket.

"Coat," he said again, "raise your right arm."

Wayne raised his right arm, and therefore, so did the coat.

"Coat, raise your left arm."

Wayne raised his left arm, and therefore, so did the coat.

"The only way this coat can do anything is if I am in it," he reiterated. "It's the same way for us in our faith walks. There's nothing that can happen in your life until Jesus gets inside of you. God has bought you. You are His. But don't you want to be the coat that God puts on every morning instead of being left hanging in the closet?"

I want to learn more about THAT, I thought to myself that morning.

I WAS BEGINNING TO UNDERSTAND that there might be a different way for me to approach my faith, my standing before God, and therefore my life—a way that was rooted in God's work rather than my own, *being* rather than *doing*, *resting* rather than *performing*.

I'm sure I had heard something similar to Wayne's teachings before, but for some reason his message struck me as fresh that morning. What happened to me that morning is something that has probably happened to most of us: sometimes you aren't ready to truly receive something in your life until you are propelled into a new realm of understanding—usually through love or suffering. I felt like I was on the brink of a fresh start—as if I had been thrust onto a new shore, like Jonah, ready to obey God and to allow the Holy Spirit to direct my paths.

> "The only way this coat can do anything is if I am in it. It's the same way for us in our faith walks. There's nothing that can happen in your life until Jesus gets inside of you. God has bought you. You are His. But don't you want to be the coat that God puts on every morning instead of being left hanging in the closet?"

Wayne's illustration took root immediately in my life. In my own spiritual paradigm, it had always been about me *performing* for God to prove my worth to Him. Just as I had performed on the football field. Just as I had performed in romantic relationships. Just as I had performed in ministry.

Listening to Wayne that morning, I was ready to receive the gift of the gospel for what it really was—and this time, I didn't want to mold it or warp it into anything else. I wanted the heart of the gospel. The idea that God might dare to wear *me* as His coat and empower *me* was freeing! Wayne seemed to be offering a spiritual paradigm to those at church that morning that was not based on performance. As Wayne had said, "It's not about what you say or don't say, what you do or don't do; it's about what Christ has already done."

I began to believe that God chose me like Wayne chose his coat. I began to believe that God bought me like Wayne purchased his coat from the store. I began to understand at a deeper, more meaningful level that God wanted to wear me as His coat, each and every day, as Wayne wore his sport coat that Sunday. I began to believe that God wanted to empower me and direct me from *within*, just as Wayne empowered and directed the movement of his coat that morning. I had been a believer for many years but had never allowed that truth to penetrate my heart until that day.

> *"I was beginning to understand that there might be a different way for me to approach my faith, my standing before God, and therefore my life—a way that was rooted in God's work rather than my own, being rather than doing, resting rather than performing."*

After the church service, I approached Wayne, introduced myself, and asked him, "Pastor Wayne, is there any chance we could get together in the next week or so? I'd love to learn more about what you were saying today during your sermon."

Little did I know that his agreement to meet with me would begin a relationship that would change my life.

In and Through

- What do you think about Wayne Barber's sermon illustration? How does it apply to your faith journey and your life right now?

- Do you believe that God would dare to live in you and through you? Why or why not?

- Do you base your spiritual standing before God on your own performance or on His performance in you and through you? How can you allow yourself to awaken more to this freeing and profound paradigm rooted in union with God?

- Read 1 Corinthians 6:19–20. What stands out to you about these verses? How do they relate to Wayne's coat analogy? How do they speak into your life today?

CHAPTER 19

Living Grace

Around the time that I began going to Wayne's church, I started breaking down my Capitalistic Christianity. A tape series and booklet that resonated with me at the time was something called *The 4 Spiritual Secrets* by Dick Woodward, founder of the Mini Bible College (MBC).

The four secrets, Woodward explained, were these:

1. *I'm not, but He is (and I'm in Him, and He is in me).*
2. *I can't, but He can (and I'm in Him, and He is in me).*
3. *I don't want to, but He wants to (and I'm in Him, and He is in me).*
4. *I didn't, but He did (because I was in Him, and He was in me).*

All of these "secrets" seemed to run contradictory to the performance-based foundation on which I had built my spirituality. In fact, if someone were to break down my approach to faith into four bullet points, it might have looked more like this:

1. *I am what I do or accomplish.*
2. *I can get close to God if I try hard enough.*
3. *I don't want to, and He is disappointed in me for not wanting to.*
4. *I didn't, and He is disappointed in me for not doing it.*

As you can see, my perception of my relationship with God was conditional. Just like everything else in my life. I thought my successes could be attributed to being good enough and that my failures could be attributed to not being good enough. But I had failed to recognize that when Jesus entered this broken world and decided to unite himself with humanity, it was a demonstration of God's love prevailing despite our sins and shortcomings.

It was becoming *real* to me that God lived in me. Though it was sometimes outrageous to even consider that Someone as perfect and pure and holy as God would unite Himself with someone like me who was filthy, imperfect, and sinful, I was beginning to take ownership of some of these truths.

It's interesting to me that the same type of message that I had first heard from Don Cockroft years before when I prayed to receive Christ was now echoing back at me: there is nothing we need to do but enjoy a relationship with God. But I had taken that initial message I had heard and somehow muddied the waters by projecting my own experiences from life—particularly my childhood experiences with my earthly father and my performance-based mindset in football and ministry—onto God and my approach to spirituality. Like the Pharisees, I had taken spirituality and muddied the waters with religion. Every true and precious gift of God that I had received throughout my life had somehow gotten warped and twisted through my performance mentality.

But my suffering had broken me down and brought me back to square one. I was ready to receive again because I was empty. It seems that we must continually empty and humbly open ourselves to new understandings or else our spirituality will become nothing more than a mask of self-righteousness or a way to look down upon others since we "have it all figured out." For me, it took crashing and burning to open myself up again to this teaching and to take my ego off the pedestal.

My first meeting with Pastor Wayne reemphasized what I was already learning from Dick Woodward's *The 4 Spiritual Secrets* and Jay's teachings. Wayne and I sat there in the quiet, comforting confines of his office at Hoffmantown Church, and he graciously listened to my story. He did not act surprised or judgmental when I told him about my infidelities or my divorce. He met me right where I was. Not only did he listen to me, but he *heard* me, which created a great feeling of being understood. He did not try to solve my problems; he entered *into* them. He did not try to dissect where I had gone wrong; he stepped into the present, into the exact place where I was. He talked to me like I was a brother, a friend. Have you ever met with someone for the first time and felt like you were going to be friends forever? That's what it was like being with Wayne.

> "It seems that we must continually empty and humbly open ourselves to new understandings or else our spirituality will become nothing more than a mask of self-righteousness or a way to look down upon others since we 'have it all figured out.'"

Wayne helped me to understand, with a big smile on his face, that God had not given up on me. He reminded me of the story of David, and how he, too, had committed adultery. And not only that, but David had also committed murder in an attempt to hide the adultery. Although there were earthly consequences for David's sin, God did not give up on him.

We agreed to continue meeting, and just about every week for the next two and a half years, Wayne sat with me and walked me through the Book of Philippians.

Wayne's teaching of Philippians was transformative for me. I guess that's a good thing since it took us two and a half years to get through it. Never had I met a teacher as personable and wise and grace-filled as Wayne before. I would often walk out of our meetings thinking to myself, *How in the world did I miss this idea in my walk with Christ?*

I don't think that Wayne was necessarily teaching "new ideas," but he was framing old ideas in a different way. He was the right person to guide me at this particular time in my life. I was finally allowing my self-worth to shift from what I did to this: resting in what God had done for me.

Wayne called it "Living Grace"—which is "Christ in me, the hope of glory" (Colossians 1:27). *Living Grace* was also the title of a book that Wayne published in 2005 and was also the name of a ministry that he eventually started. I think that Wayne was passionate about encouraging others to live in the reality of God's grace because he had seen so many Christians burn-out trying to hold themselves to a level of perfection that was unattainable—and therefore strapping themselves to shackles of guilt and shame when they failed.

> *"I was finally allowing my self-worth to shift from what I did to this: resting in what God had done for me."*

When I shared with Wayne some of my struggles with temptation and sin, he would often say to me in that deep Tennessee accent and Southern drawl, "Boy, did you think that your flesh was getting better?"

"Well, I've been a believer for more twenty years, so I think *some* things ought to be getting better," I remember telling him.

"Son," he said, smiling, "the Scriptures teach us that our flesh is getting older and uglier and more deceptive, and that's why we need to let Jesus be Jesus in us."

Wayne wasn't making an excuse for our fleshly desires; rather, he was suggesting that we have grace for ourselves in our humanity and awaken more and more to the reality of our profound union with God.

Basically he was saying that I was trying too hard, relying too much on myself, and believing everything was up to me and my performance. My standing before God was far more profound than something as human-based as a performance checklist.

Reading through the Book of Philippians—a letter from the Apostle Paul to the church of Philippi—with Wayne through the lens of Living Grace quickly made Philippians a sort of "life book" for me and the direction that I wanted to take in my life. The Bible's words began to become more living and active than ever before.

Wayne broke Philippians down into the four cornerstones at the foundation of our faith.

The first cornerstone is **The New Life** and is based off Philippians 1:6: "For I am confident of this very thing, that He who began a good work in you will perfect it until the day of Christ Jesus."

Wayne taught me that the whole idea that Paul was portraying in this verse is that God starts the work in us, perfects the work in us, and finishes the work in us. When I became a Christian in high school, I understood my need for a savior, and as I continued to explore my faith, I always understood my need for a savior because I was always in touch with my sin—my failings, my performance. But I had always thought that I had more to do with the sanctification process in my life than God did. I believed that it was all up to me and my own strength—not God's strength *in* me. Wayne explained the faith walk in the context of Living Grace as more of a partnership: my job was to pick up my foot in faith and then allow and rely on God to place my foot down, wherever He wanted to place it.

The second cornerstone in Philippians is **The Attitude Towards**

New Life, which further unpacks what New Life entails.

Chapter 2 begins with these verses:

> *Therefore if there is any encouragement in Christ, if there is any consolation of love, if there is any fellowship of the Spirit, if any affection and compassion, make my joy complete by being of the same mind, maintaining the same love, united in spirit, intent on one purpose. Do nothing from selfishness or empty conceit, but with humility of mind regard one another as more important than yourselves; do not merely look out for your own personal interests, but also for the interests of others. Have this attitude in yourselves which was also in Christ Jesus, who, although He existed in the form of God, did not regard equality with God a thing to be grasped, but emptied Himself, taking the form of a bond-servant, and being made in the likeness of men.*

Much of Chapter 2, Wayne taught me, is a reflection of these verses, as Paul explains what it means to be "united with Christ." Selflessness. Humility. Servanthood. Obedience. Sacrifice. And yet, it is not *us* working to attain these things, as if to check tasks off a checklist; it's Christ's work in us and through us. We only need to be willing to abide in this reality. As Philippians 2:12–13 says, "So then, my beloved, just as you have always obeyed, not as in my presence only, but now much more in my absence, work out your salvation with fear and trembling; for it is God who is at work *in you*, both to will and to work for His good pleasure" (italics added). Wayne helped me understand that in the original Greek, Paul was essentially saying, "That which God put in you, let God work it out of you"—a continued thread throughout the book of Philippians.

The third cornerstone, as Wayne explained it, is **The Goal of the New Life.**

Finally. Now I can set a goal and then accomplish that goal, I thought to myself.

The flagship verse that Wayne pointed to was 3:14: "I press on toward the goal to win the prize for which God has called me heavenward in Christ Jesus." Paul had laid his resumé out on the table earlier in the letter—as if applying for a job—and said that he considers every item on that list *loss* for the sake of Christ. Right when I thought the narrative was going to take a turn and dive into the "performance" aspect of Christianity, Paul actually went the opposite way and said that all of his achievements—all his perceived righteousness—was loss!

Wayne explained to me that the primary goal of the Christian life is to press into a relationship with Christ, something that only reaffirmed what Jay had shared with me: that God wanted to be my friend. The goal was to rest in my perfect union with God and to live out of that reality. When Wayne explained to me the nature of this "goal," I thought to myself, *Really? That's it?*

> *"I was beginning to understand that living the Christian life was not so much about working hard to attain God's favor but was rather about living out of the incomprehensible favor that already existed. Faith was not so much about striving, but rather about living out of a place of rest and contentment—abiding."*

The fourth cornerstone is **The Strength to Live the Life**. The core verse, 4:13, is one that is very popular: "I press on toward the goal for the prize of the upward call of God in Christ Jesus."

So, in conclusion, God starts the work, perfects the work, and finishes the work (Chapter 1); our union with Him helps us to be humble, sacrificial, and obedient (Chapter 2); the goal of the Christian life is to press into a relationship with Him (Chapter 3); and we can live a meaningful life like this because He gives us strength to do so (Chapter 4).

I WAS BEGINNING TO UNDERSTAND that living the Christian life was not so much about working hard to attain God's favor but was rather about living out of the incomprehensible favor that already existed. Faith was not so much about striving, but rather about living out of a place of rest and contentment—*abiding*. Following Jesus was not so much about being in a relationship with Him that was constantly fluctuating like most of my romantic relationships, but was about being in *union* with God through the mystery of the Holy Spirit, and living out of that fullness and wholeness.

Wayne's patience as he walked me through a two-and-a-half-year study of Philippians helped me to gracefully transition into a new spiritual paradigm once and for all. And Wayne did more than spend time with me in the Word; we also grew a deep friendship that included frequently hunting and fishing together.

Most importantly, I began to experience the incomprehensible reality of God's love and acceptance.

As I mentioned in the introduction, Wayne Barber sadly passed away right when I was beginning this book. I will truly miss my conversations with him, but I look forward to the promise that I have in Christ Jesus that I'll see him again.

And in the meantime, I know one thing: that Wayne's teachings will help me to continue to live out of a heaven-focused mentality here on earth.

Striving vs. Abiding

- Do you ever feel guilt or shame in your walk with Christ? Explain.

- Have you experienced exhaustion or burnout in your walk with Christ? Explain.

- How does this statement make you feel: "God loves you for who you are, not for who you should be"?

- Compare striving and abiding. How are you striving in your relationship with God right now? How are you abiding and resting?

- Reread these verses in Philippians: 1:6, 2:1–2, 3:14, and 4:13. What can you learn from these verses and Wayne's application of Paul's epistle to the Philippians?

CHAPTER 20
The Father I Never Knew

For legalistic Christians, this idea of divine union—of God living in us and through us—can be a complicated one, because it shifts the focus from our own work to the work of God in our lives. The modern-day Pharisee hates to believe that we are complete and worthy without doing anything at all. It was certainly difficult for me to believe, and it is still sometimes hard for me to accept today when my works-based tendencies creep back up.

But once we allow God to live in us and through us, sanctification begins. And the interesting thing about sanctification is that it involves some of the most difficult decisions in the Christian walk. Some people think that becoming a Christian is the most difficult decision to make, and sometimes it is, but for me it meant letting go of my tendencies and allowing sanctification to run its course.

During this period of my life, this sanctification process seemed to reveal itself in three major ways: parenting, relationships, and work....

I hated what I put my daughters through—in the way I treated them and through the divorce. Though my ex-wife and I had shared custody, I decided not to force them to stay with me. Our daughters didn't volunteer to be in our family, and they certainly didn't cause the divorce, so I decided not to force their lives to be uprooted or disrupted. I'm unsure if I would've been able to "let go" in this way had I not been trying to live out of this new spiritual paradigm.

I think my daughters appreciated this freedom, and they consequently each decided—at one point—to live with me. Though I still implemented rules, they were rules that they agreed on before they moved in. They were nowhere as strict as the rules I'd imposed on them throughout the majority of their childhoods. I wanted them to make my house their home.

Living Grace was being applied to my life in parenting. This is what a continual, evolving understanding of divine grace naturally does: it gently infiltrates every avenue of our lives.

That said, I found myself entering into a *friendship* with my daughters.

One day, for example, one of my daughters hesitantly approached me and tearfully confessed to me about a mistake she had made.

"Dad, do you hate me?" she asked fearfully.

"Absolutely not, sweetie," I told her. "I love you. There's nothing you could do that would ever change that."

She hugged me, and we had one of the most precious moments a father and daughter could have.

"The beauty of our faith in Christ is that every day is a new morning," I told her. "God sees us cleansed. Every day, we get to start over. Right now, God sees you as a perfect, blameless child who is loved and forgiven."

> *"The more I began to believe that God really liked me and loved me, regardless of my performance, the more this love seemed to spill over into other aspects of my life."*

I could only say something like this because of the shame and humiliation that I too had experienced in failure. Years before in my Pharisaic mind, what my daughter told me might have sent me into an angry and condemning tirade. But not now. I was learning to enter into my daughters' struggles, just as Christ had entered into mine. Boy, isn't it good news that we can get a little better?

My more graceful approach to parenting was evidence of Living Grace's movement. The more I began to believe that God *really* liked me and loved me, regardless of my performance, the more this love seemed to spill over into other aspects of my life. I wanted to share this with my daughters.

Another area where sanctification continued to run its course was in the relationship avenue of my life.

I knew one thing: I didn't want to be a single man the rest of my life. God had not given me a heart for celibacy. I don't think my deep desire to be with someone was a bad desire (after all, even God says that it is "not good for man to be alone" in the Genesis narrative), but it was an insecurity nonetheless—a craving that sometimes led to decisions that were not exactly healthy for me. A relationship for me was always a crutch, a security blanket. I've always been a needy person when it comes to relationships.

I was afraid to enter into that space—that void—where I allowed God to fill those needs of mine for approval and affection. Looking back, I can see that my discomfort in being alone and unattached—which was ultimately me not allowing God's grace to be sufficient for me—was a pattern in my life that led to toxic decision-making, heartache, and troubles.

I was beginning to decide that I wanted a new melody. Relationally speaking, I felt that I had been telling myself a false story—that I needed something more than God, that God wasn't enough, and that I could fill that void by finding a soulmate. And ultimately, I felt like I needed something more because I didn't trust God with the miraculous—that he could lead a divorcee like me into another marriage.

In the well-known biblical story where Jesus meets the Samaritan woman at the well, Jesus famously says to the adulterous woman, "Go get your husband." Jesus knew that the woman had many husbands—men who she was sleeping with. Jesus's meeting with this woman was culturally taboo, but Jesus told her that her baggage, insecurities, and inner darkness did not scare him. He was basically saying, "Bring it all and surrender it to me so that I can deal with it."

In my own life, I sometimes seemed to have a "buffet mentality" on what I could and couldn't surrender. I would pick and choose what I wanted to hold onto. Though I was willing to let go and surrender some things, there were other things that I carefully guarded. I really struggled to surrender my romantic life and the void of my loneliness to God.

But ever so slowly, I was learning to surrender different things.

At around this time, there was a series of events that got me think-ing about moving to Las Vegas, of all places. I wanted to get out of my comfort zone. I only knew a few people there, two of them being Jud Wilhite and Mike Bodine, who were pastors at Central Church. And on two consecutive weekends, I visited the church they were pastoring, and I was moved both times. Pastor Jud's messages stirred something in my heart.

This desire to move to Las Vegas led me to the third primary facet in my life where sanctification was unfolding: my professional life, an area that had always hinged on my performance and my ability to control situations.

I became very aware of my tendency to force circumstances into existence to get what I wanted. I was always a "make it happen" kind of guy when it came to growing the work that I was involved in. If I thought something was worth going after, I worked hard to achieve it—even if it meant micromanagement and control. (It's always more difficult to keep your ego in check when you are actually passionate about what you are doing.)

Working at ICM wasn't just another nine-to-five job for me. It felt incredible to be back working in ministry. Not only that, but I felt that ICM was the best-kept ministry secret in the country. I loved that each day afforded me an opportunity to help raise money for a ministry that was helping to build churches in broken communities all around the world. But I was becoming aware of my controlling tendencies and was being challenged, through the process of sanctification, to surrender more and more.

Over time, just as I had begun to see how comfortable it was for me to remain in a relationship even if it wasn't going to lead to marriage, I also began to see how comfortable it was for me to remain in New Mexico. I was well-networked there, which was vital for what I was doing with ICM. This is another reason why I was hesitant to move.

But after five years of working at ICM in Albuquerque and being changed and molded as Living Grace began to infiltrate every aspect of my life, something within me made me feel compelled to move. I had exhausted my connections in Albuquerque, and not only that, I felt like I was still relying on myself. Sometimes it felt like I was still the one getting things done rather than watching God put it together. That performance-based thing again.

I wanted to move away. I wanted to move somewhere where I had to rely entirely on God, not on myself. I wanted to truly experience my faith and depend on God in a profound way.

The idea of moving to Las Vegas became a reality. I could not deny how inspiring those two weekends had been in attending the church that Jud and Mike pastored. Something about the city seemed to call me to it.

By this time, my daughters were in college and moving into the next phase of their lives. I was single, and Dois had given me the freedom to work remotely. Why *wouldn't* I move away in a display of faith? I wanted God to know that I trusted Him. Anyone who has felt that they should move away might be able to relate. It doesn't necessarily make practical sense, but there is something within you urging you to do so.

I knew it would be difficult to leave New Mexico. Albuquerque was home to me. Yes, some of my biggest struggles unfolded in Albuquerque, but it's also where I became who I am today—where I went to school, raised a family, played a part in an impactful ministry, and encountered the God of Living Grace.

But I knew that it was time to move on.

I WAS BEGINNING TO UNDERSTAND that I needed to allow this loving Father—this new understanding of the Christian God—to permeate every avenue of my life. My approach in three avenues of my life—parenting, relationships, and work—was rubbing up against this new spiritual paradigm that Wayne had introduced to me. My old tendencies were colliding with Living Grace.

It seems that the areas of our lives that are the most important to us are often those in which we struggle the most to surrender to God's sanctification process.

I had been given a new picture of a Father, a father I'd never known, a loving father as exemplified in Jesus's famous parable of the Prodigal Son. A father who *ran* toward and *pursued* the lost son, despite the fact that he had squandered his inheritance. A father who *embraced* the lost son and threw a party for him. A father who also pursued the self-righteous son with the same fervor and undying love.

It will be impossible to ever fully understand God's character, but it's vital for our understanding of Him to be rooted in love, a love that is exemplified in the person of Jesus Christ.

There I was, in the second half of my life, reconstructing the foundation of my God-view. And it was up to me to allow that sanctifying love to infuse *everything*.

An approach to sanctification that is rooted in Living Grace frees us from a performance-based spirituality, which is dependent on the strength of our own will and actions, and shifts the process toward an awareness of what is true. This God of unfathomable love wanted to encompass all my identity and all my life. This even included my mistakes and the times when I slipped back into my old tendencies. I am typically ultracritical of my mistakes and hard on myself when I fail, but Living Grace meant extending grace to myself as I allowed God to break down my lifelong tendencies and formulas. The God of love was sanctifying me and constantly meeting me where I was in my transformation.

> "An approach to sanctification that is rooted in Living Grace frees us from a performance-based spirituality, which is dependent on the strength of our own will and actions, and shifts the process toward an awareness of what is true."

When we are becoming "sanctified," we are eventually challenged to take a big risk. It was time for me to move.

The Movement of Living Grace

- What are some of your tendencies in your approach to parenting/family, relationships, work, or anything else that is important to you? Where do you think those tendencies come from?

- How can you allow the idea of a loving, gentle Father to permeate the deepest concerns of your life? What areas of your life has Living Grace yet to infiltrate?

- Read Luke 15:11–32. Put yourself in the shoes of the lost son. If you were returning home, what would make you hang your head? What in your life has led to your shame? Now picture the father running out to meet you on the road, embracing you, and then throwing a party for you. Meditate on this image. What stands out to you about this story?

CHAPTER 21
Sin City & Surrender

The great thing about sanctification is that it makes you more and more secure in your relationship with Christ because you become more in touch with who you are, which is Christ in you. When I moved to Las Vegas, I was finally okay with myself and who I was. My identity suddenly seemed to breach deeper than who I was with romantically—or even if I was with anyone at all. I surrendered my future to God. I wanted to find a spouse, but I was done trying to control and micromanage the process. Similarly, my identity suddenly breached deeper than my professional comforts in Albuquerque that flowed from my extensive network of friends and connections and donors. I surrendered my work at ICM to God.

It was as if I was finally beginning to understand what it meant to "let go and let God."

When we surrender that which we've been holding onto with clenched fists, our posture of openness shows God that we are willing to trust Him and partner with Him. Returning to the biblical story about Jesus and the Samaritan woman: it was as if God was meeting me at the well, too. He was asking me to bring all my insecurities and surrender them to Him so that He could deal with them. And the more I did this, the more I seemed to be in touch with my truest self.

> *"The great thing about sanctification is that it makes you more and more secure in your relationship with Christ because you become more in touch with who you are, which is Christ in you."*

I was beginning to understand who I was.

I was becoming more confident in who I was.

And I wanted to surrender everything to the Lord.

So I decided to move to Las Vegas as a personal demonstration of this surrender.

God was calling me further into the wilderness, calling me to move to Vegas without any attachments. To enter into the unknown. To enter into the desert, which I suppose was both physical and metaphorical. To Las Vegas—Sin City, the place known around the world for the saying, "What happens in Vegas stays in Vegas."

Once my move was official, I immediately began to see God's hand working in my life.

First, on a personal level.

I knew it'd be strange and scary to go from a community where I could walk into just about any establishment and know a handful of people to suddenly being surrounded by strangers. There is a great comfort in being connected. It makes you feel like you have some sense of control.

When my nephew-in-law, Lew, found out that I was moving, he reached out to me and told me that his mother lived in Las Vegas. I had never even met his mother, but he said that she was going to Europe for a month and that she would love for me to stay at her house and watch over everything if I didn't have a place to stay.

I decided to take Lew up on the offer. Living at his mom's house gave me a month to decide where I was going to live long-term. Before he reached out, I'd planned on living in one of those week-by-week hotels until I figured out my situation and got on my feet. That might sound haphazard or sudden, but I didn't want to delay moving to a place where I knew I was supposed to go. I had come to a place of surrender and didn't want to suppress the call that I knew I'd heard. The easiest thing to do when one hears a call is to delay the decision. A few years before, I probably would have wanted to figure out the details before I moved. But all I felt from God in this phase of my life was: "Go."

So I went.

The only negative thing about Lew's mother's house was that she didn't have Internet access, so I went to a nearby Starbucks each day to get my work done. Now, this Starbucks wasn't your typical Starbucks. It was massive and was somewhat of a gathering place in the community. It didn't even have a drive-up window because people who went to this Starbucks always stayed there for a while. It was the way coffee shops used to be in Europe—a place where people gathered to discuss issues, bounce ideas off of one another, and enter into fellowship. All that being said, it was sometimes difficult to find a place to sit, especially in the morning.

One day, I saw a pair of comfortable chairs in the corner and asked the woman who was sitting in one of them if anyone was sitting next to her. She said no, so I set my computer down while I got my tea.

When I returned, she said to me, "Gosh, isn't it too cold to be wearing shorts?"

It was December, and I had just finished working out at the gym. I was wearing shorts and a jacket.

"Yeah, I just moved here from New Mexico, and I didn't realize that it got this cold here in Vegas," I laughed.

"What do you do?" she then asked.

"I work out of my house for an organization," I told her. "I'm living at my nephew's mother's house right now."

"Around here?"

"Yeah, right over there, just a mile or so away," I pointed, "off a street called Sterling Heights."

She gave me a funny look and said, "When you leave here, do you go in the first gate or the second gate?"

It became apparent that she lived off of Sterling Heights as well.

"The second gate," I said.

"What's the gate code?" she laughed, as if to make sure that I wasn't messing with her.

I told her the gate code.

"Which house?"

I told her which house.

"You're kidding me!" she exclaimed. "I know exactly where you live. You live right across the street from me!"

We talked for a while more, and I found myself attracted to her. Her name was Cathy. She was intelligent, friendly, beautiful, and single. She said that she was a pharmaceutical representative in the area and that she had lived in Vegas for many years.

After finishing her coffee, she told me that she had to leave but handed me her business card. "If you have any questions about the area, feel free to give me a call," she said. She was only being nice. By no means did I feel like she was being forward.

I watched her walk out of the Starbucks and said to myself, *I'm giving it two days, and I'm calling her.*

> "It seems that we first must step into the void of our insecurities if we ever want God to fill them. And He almost always fills them in very unexpected ways."

Here I was, in Vegas, in the process of surrendering my relational and romantic insecurities to God, and He dropped this nice lady into my world.

I gave it two days, and then I gave her a call. Over time, Cathy and I began hanging out and building a friendship.

It seems that we first must step into the void of our insecurities if we ever want God to fill them.

And He almost always fills them in very unexpected ways.

Secondly, I immediately saw God's hand working on a ministry level in Las Vegas. One might wonder: Why would you move to Las Vegas, of all places, for ministry? But the truth is that Las Vegas was the fastest-growing Christian community per capita in the United States at the time. And one of the things I found to be true in Vegas was that there was a true dividing line between right and wrong. It was very clear that it was the way of the world versus the way of God.

When it came to my job, my success at ICM depended entirely on my network and how I could educate people about the opportunity to assist believers in developing countries in a much-needed way. In this sense, there was vast opportunity in Vegas because I was exposed to an entirely new group of people and connections. In another sense, there was a huge risk involved because I was stepping away from the sustainability I had established in New Mexico. It was much harder to manage that network from so far away.

But I knew that I had no time to waste. I needed to put myself out there and do anything I could to make connections early on. This was the equivalent of what Wayne had always talked about: me picking up my foot and allowing God to place it wherever He wished.

The week before I moved, I had called a man named Dean McQuillan, the FCA state director of Nevada, just to introduce myself to him and let him know that I was moving to Las Vegas. I told him about my background in football and in ministry and about how I had come to know the Lord through FCA.

"Could you come to Vegas a day early and come to our annual FCA banquet?" he asked me.

I told him I could and moved a day early to be there, where I met Dean for the first time. We had a nice talk, and he thanked me for coming. He eventually led me to my seat, which was situated at a table facing the doorway to the auditorium. As I sat at the table alone, I kept a close eye on each person who entered the ballroom. I like to people-watch.

One thing I noticed as I observed the scene was that there were signs *everywhere* with the word "Findlay" on them. Findlay Toyota. Findlay Chevrolet. Findlay Automotive. Findlay this. Findlay that. (This seems like an unnecessary detail right now but is something that I will return to later.)

Several minutes went by, and I eventually locked eyes with someone as he walked through the doorway. He looked extremely familiar to me, and as he approached my table, I recognized that it was Randall Birk, a youth pastor in Las Vegas who I happened to know from Albuquerque. We began to talk. I asked Randall who "Findlay" was, and he told me that a man named Rich Abajian was the general manager at Findlay and the primary sponsor for the event. He also told me that Mr. Abajian was a strong Christian and one of the most influential people in Las Vegas.

As we talked, I saw another familiar face. It was Dwaine Knight, the former head golf coach at the University of New Mexico and the current coach at the University of Nevada, Las Vegas. Dwaine was one of the best golf coaches in the country. Tiger Woods had wanted to play for him at UNLV, but Tiger's dad didn't want his son going to college in Sin City. Understandable, I guess.

Turns out, Dwaine was the guest speaker at the event. After the banquet, I approached him.

"Randy Rich!" he said, extending his hand towards me. "What are you doing here?"

"Coach," I smiled, shaking his hand, "I just moved here."

"Listen," he told me, "you need to come over to the athletic department next week. The new head coach is a strong Christian, and I'd love to connect the two of you."

I called Dwaine on Monday, and he invited me to meet him on campus on Tuesday. There Dwaine introduced me to one of the assistant coaches for UNLV football. He was the only one there, as the rest of the staff was out recruiting. I gave the coach my card and told him to contact me if there was anything I could ever do to help with the program.

The next day, Wednesday—the same day that I first met Cathy at Starbucks—I received a call from the assistant coach at UNLV.

"Randy, remember when you came in yesterday and told me that if there was anything that you could do to help me to give you a call?"

"Of course," I laughed. It had only been a day, and he was already calling me.

"Well, I've got a dilemma," he continued. "I've got a high school football banquet that I've been asked to speak at. Without thinking about it, I said yes. But I just realized that I can't do it because it would violate recruiting rules. Have you ever spoken at sports banquets?"

"Absolutely," I told him. "I've done plenty of them."

"Could you speak at it?" he asked.

"Of course," I said. "When is it?"

"Tonight," he laughed.

It was one o'clock in the afternoon. The banquet was at six.

"I can absolutely do it," I told him. "I've got nothing to do. I'll be there."

As silly and last-minute as it was, I couldn't help but wonder if God was at work.

So I went to the banquet at this nearby public school on a whim and introduced myself to the high school football coach, a man who had been coaching at the school for twenty-eight years or something like that—he was the Turk Eliades of Las Vegas.

"I wasn't sure if you were going to show up, so I got someone else to speak, too," the coach said. "Is that okay? Both of you can speak."

"Coach," I said, "I don't even need to speak today if you don't need me to."

"No, no, that's all right," he assured.

Their coach guided me to a table where the other speaker, a big African-American man who I recognized from somewhere, was sitting.

"Hi there," I said, "my name is Randy Rich."

"Hi, I'm Ed O'Bannon," he said to me, extending his hand.

I immediately recognized the name.

"*The* Ed O'Bannon?" I asked. "The O'Bannon brothers?"

Turns out, I had followed Ed and his brother's basketball careers for a few years. They had both played at UCLA and had each been drafted into the NBA.

"I've followed your career," I told him. "It's an honor to meet you."

I spoke first at the banquet, and when it was Ed's turn, he simply took the podium and said, "Coach, for me to come up here and say anything more would be redundant. Mr. Rich shared everything that is important. I want to congratulate all of you on a great year in football." And that was pretty much all he said.

It was actually kind of embarrassing at the time because my intention wasn't to put a fellow athlete in an awkward position. But now it is just a funny story.

After the banquet, Ed said to me, "Randy, it sounds like you have an interesting story. I'd love to get to know you."

"I don't know anyone here, Ed," I said. "I'd love to get together sometime."

Ed handed me his business card. It read:

Ed O'Bannon
Sales Manager
Findlay Toyota

Here I was, in Vegas, having just surrendered my work at ICM to the Lord, and He dropped this unlikely strand of events into my world. Isn't it so amazing how God delights in directing every aspect of our lives?

Ed ended up introducing me to Rich Abajian, the general manager of Findlay, and Rich sponsored a number of ICM church plants around the world.

Isn't God amazing?

I WAS BEGINNING TO UNDERSTAND that I had never had control of my life to begin with. I don't want to go on and on with story after story of God's revelations to me in Las Vegas because the truth is that to include every story would require another book in itself. But the point is that in Las Vegas, I began to understand how "in control" God was of my life. Dick Woodward's spiritual truths were becoming my reality: *I'm not, but He is; I can't, but He can; I don't want to, but He wants to; I didn't, but He did.*

It wasn't all up to me and my performance after all. For perhaps the first time in my life, I was realizing what it actually meant to walk by faith. Though I always gave God the credit for things that happened throughout my radio career in New Mexico, it was as if I was ultimately giving gratitude to God for what I had done, not for what He had done, believing all along that the success of the station was all up to me.

But in Las Vegas, it was impossible for me to take the credit for anything. I met Cathy on my fifth day in Vegas. I met a man who would introduce to me to someone who would become one of ICM's primary donors that same day. And I went on to know as many people in Las Vegas as I did in New Mexico. It was if God was gently saying to me, "Son, you've never been in control. You thought you were, but I've always been leading you and directing you. You need to let go, Randy. You need to completely let go."

> *"I had long held onto both my personal life and professional life with clenched fists. But God was helping me to slowly open up my hands as a form of surrender so that I could taste freedom. So that I could live out of the sufficiency of His grace and love. So that I could awaken to contentment, even when I felt like I had no control at all."*

I had long held onto both my personal life and professional life with clenched fists. But God was helping me to slowly open up my hands as a form of surrender so that I could taste freedom. So that I could live out of the sufficiency of His grace and love. So that I could awaken to contentment, even when I felt like I had no control at all.

After that first week in Las Vegas, I started waking up each morning and praying, "God, who are we going to meet today? How will it tie into the incredible things You are doing in ICM and around the world and even in my life?" Each day had a magic to it. A grace to it. An ease to it. The more I opened my fists to receive God's blessings, the more peace I felt, and the more in awe I stood of God's wondrous hand on my life—His indwelling in me.

One thing was becoming very apparent: the Christian life had a lot more to do with allowing God to do His work in me and through me than exhausting myself doing things for God and attempting to control my life, always grasping at peace and stability and comfort.

Letting Go

- What are you struggling to let go of in this life? What are you proverbially holding in your palms? Does it have to do with your personal life? Your professional life? Past pain or bitterness? Future angst or uncertainty? Think about these things. Close your eyes, clench your fists, and enter into silent meditation.

- Keeping your eyes closed and fists clenched, slowly open up your hands. What issues in your life are rising from your hands? What are you surrendering? Think about these things.

- Be honest with yourself. Though you might have done the above exercise, what were you struggling to surrender? What are your fears in surrendering these issues? Picture God, the Father, running toward you and meeting you where you are in those fears. Jesus's words in Matthew 6 reveal that he understood that fear and worry are natural feelings in the human experience. What does it mean to you that God understands your struggles as well as the difficulties of surrender?

- Read Matthew 6:25–34. Why was Jesus saying these things to the people of his day? Read the verses again. What rises to the surface as you think about these verses in the context of your own life?

CHAPTER 22
To Die, To Live

I can't tell you how instrumental the next three years in Las Vegas were for me in my Christian walk. It was a real progression of learning to trust and depend on God more than ever before. Wayne Barber's coat analogy became a reality for me.

Personally, I became healthier and no longer relied on my performance. Spiritually, God became more real because I saw His tangible involvement in my life. And professionally, ICM grew exponentially because of the resources our team stumbled upon under God's direction and the network of people that He brought into the ministry.

Relationally, I felt like I had really found someone with whom I wanted to spend the rest of my life in Cathy. There's something about down-to-earth Texas gals, I guess. She was grounded, level-headed, consistent, intelligent, and compassionate. She brought a balance into my life that I believed would make for a great marriage. I'm a visionary; she is logical. I'm emotional; she is practical. I found our blend of outlooks and personalities to be extremely healthy, because I can get really excited about things, which helps us to move forward and consider risks, but then she can bring it down to reality, pose great questions, and push the "pause" button so that we can develop a realistic plan of action together. I'm not saying this works in harmony all the time, but it's certainly what works best.

What became obvious to me in Las Vegas was that God was in the business of redeeming my brokenness. Divorce shatters a person's life, but if you surrender and take your grief and pain to the Lord, He takes you on a new journey—providing new opportunities in work and relationships, and, most importantly, enabling you to grow personally. God builds and provides the hope that any loving father wants for his kids.

By no means do I want to sound like I had arrived—personally, spiritually, professionally, relationally (in many ways, you realize how much your struggles and tendencies are still intact when sanctification is running its course)—but Las Vegas certainly presented me with the opportunity to apply what I had learned about Living Grace in my own life and to share it with others. God gave me an amazing opportunity to minister to people in Las Vegas, something I hadn't experienced in a while. I was no longer being so hard on myself and was capturing some of what it means to be totally forgiven.

I WAS BEGINNING TO UNDERSTAND that God was not so much interested in making me pay for my mistakes but rather was in the business of performing a resurrection out of my brokenness. He wasn't interested in my "I can do it" Christianity. He was more interested in "He can do it" Christianity. Yes, I had made mistakes in my life—pivotal mistakes that had severely affected the people who were closest to me. But God was teaching me that all things were possible, even through my failure.

And this is true for all of us.

We are not defined by our pasts; we have hope for the future. In Christ, we are *worthy*. We are his sons and daughters. His treasure. His prize. His friends. His saints.

> "I was beginning to understand that God was not so much interested in making me pay for my mistakes but rather was in the business of performing a resurrection out of my brokenness. He wasn't interested in my 'I can do it' Christianity. He was more interested in 'He can do it' Christianity."

God wasn't through with me. God wasn't finished with me.

The Bible is full of stories in which broken people—people who had made big mistakes in their lives—became prophets and disciples and saints. I'm not saying that's my story, by any means, but I am saying that I'm a broken person through whom God has worked. From King David, who was guilty of adultery and murder but was still described as a "man after God's own heart"; to Peter, who was guilty of denying Christ but went on to become one of the primary founders of the early church after Christ's death; to Paul, who was guilty of persecuting Christians and even killing them but went on to write some of the most profound letters in the Bible and grow the early church—the Bible is full of redemptive stories that began with brokenness.

One thing seems certain to me: God never gives up on His beloved sons and daughters. There is no situation that is beyond Him, no person that He discards as useless or worthless. He resurrects. He redeems. He restores. Through it all, no matter what we have done, no matter what mistakes we have made, He *loves* us. He is always running toward us, pursuing us. That includes me and you.

The Gospel Mystery

- Locate and name the broken places in your own life. How do you think that God feels about these broken places? How can you partner with God in moving toward redemption?

- What is strapped more tightly to your identity: your sinfulness or your "belovedness"? Your insufficiency or your "enough-ness"?

- Read Luke 24 about Christ's resurrection, as something so bleak as sin and death was conquered. What do you need to die to in order to experience rebirth/redemption/resurrection?

CHAPTER 23

Anniversary

I couldn't see myself settling in Las Vegas. After three years there, I sensed that it was time for me to move. As I mentioned before, my position at ICM allowed me the freedom to move anywhere, and it really felt like it was time to go. Oh, there was another thing: I really didn't want to endure another hot summer in Vegas.

My plan was to move to Denver, a place that Cathy could see herself settling as well, and to discover a new network of people to continue building up ICM—as I felt that God had prompted me to do in Las Vegas. I was beginning to enjoy this "surrender" thing, because it helped me to open my eyes more to God's work in the world and what He was doing in my life. I was excited to begin another chapter in Denver in my work at ICM.

I had been with ICM for nearly nine years at that point, and I'd been continually blown away by the opportunities that God had brought our way. I didn't see myself leaving that ministry anytime soon. Since joining ICM, I had enjoyed the privilege of traveling to multiple developing countries in Asia, Africa, Eastern Europe, and South America. I'd also gotten to work with number of contemporary Christian radio stations, which, as you can imagine, I particularly enjoyed. That included K-LOVE/Air1, the largest Christian radio network in the world.

> *"I was beginning to enjoy this 'surrender' thing, because it helped me to open my eyes more to God's work in the world and what He was doing in my life."*

The people at K-LOVE *loved* ICM, and they were especially fond of Dois, who, to this day, *still* works six days a week at ICM—and he's ninety-three years old! At ICM, we had a special partnership with K-LOVE, where they would allow us to participate in their daylong fundraising drives. Every year, K-LOVE takes certain days throughout the year and dedicates them to exposing their audience to ministries that most have not heard of in an effort to raise funds for viable ministries around the country. It was a real blessing for ICM to be one of those ministries. Over 114 ICM churches have been funded through K-LOVE thanks to the "Share-a-thons" they've allowed us to participate in.

Each time I worked with K-LOVE, I missed working in the radio industry; however, I felt that my ship in contemporary Christian music had sailed. It had been a good chapter of my life, but I thought it was over. I felt like I had too many scars and wounds and had caused too many scars and wounds to get back into that avenue of ministry. Looking back, that was my false self speaking again, but it was indeed how I felt at the time.

Around this time, when Cathy and I were thinking about moving to Denver, ICM's partnership with K-LOVE afforded me the opportunity to attend a K-LOVE Cruise with two of K-LOVE's executives, CEO Mike Novak and the Chief Officer of Creativity David Pierce. During that week, we talked about other ways that ICM and K-LOVE could partner with each other, along with other business opportunities. Mike was also curious to learn more about some of the community outreach programs I had been a part of in Albuquerque.

As Mike and I talked, I thought I was just giving him ideas about some of the things they could do in their ministry. But weeks later, Mike reached back out to me and asked if I would consider leading K-LOVE's new philanthropy department at their headquarters in Sacramento, California. The role of those in the department was to build relationships with capacity donors and explore how their resources could impact communities around the country.

In other words, he was offering me a job.

I was shocked.

As I mentioned, I had planned on never returning to the Christian music world. But there I was, being offered a job at the largest Christian radio network in the world. Twenty-three million listeners on a weekly basis for both networks. Nearly nine hundred signals across the country.

And they were talking to *me*—someone who had fallen from ministry—about becoming the vice president of their philanthropy department?

The opportunity was the last thing that I'd expected.

When I'd left KLYT years before, I'd grieved it as a loss and had accepted that I'd never get back into that realm of ministry. Not to mention I was really excited about the work I was doing at ICM and how I was seeing God move around the world.

I thought to myself, *Is it possible that the thing I thought I'd never be a part of again is suddenly on my doorstep?* Man, God is good.

I've always believed that music has a unique way of ministering to people—it can cross political and social barriers and speak directly into people's lives, people's souls. It seems that music, perhaps more than any other art form, can bring hope into brokenness. And radio stations can meet people where they are at any time of the day or night. You never know when a song might speak to someone. During my years working at KLYT, I had heard thousands of encouraging stories about the impact that Christian music had on people's lives. It's no surprise to me that some have suggested, based on Ezekiel 28, that Lucifer was the choir director in heaven. Music seems to be a battleground for good and evil because it is an arena where true impact, for the better or for the worse, can take place.

I was a little fearful to accept the position, but my excitement overruled my fear. I say "fear" because I think I was allowing my previous performance (and failure) in the realm of radio ministry to define me. I had a bit of an uneasy feeling of, "What are people going to think?"

But after going back and forth with Mike, getting Dois's blessing, and talking it over with Cathy, I decided to accept the position as the vice president of philanthropy at K-LOVE/Air1 and move to Sacramento, California. I never thought that I'd move back to the land of the fruits and nuts. But there I was.

Is this really happening?

On the morning of June 6, 2010, I pulled onto K-LOVE's Sacramento campus for my first day of work.

In some ways, it was an overwhelming task to return to radio in this way and to lead the philanthropy team—but I welcomed the challenge. After all, I had been working solely by myself for many years, and I was being asked to lead a team. And I couldn't help but think about how I had run our team at KLYT—with a hard fist. I wanted to do it differently at K-LOVE. I wanted to be a gracious leader. I didn't want to diminish my standards, but I wanted to lead with gentleness and mercy.

Sometimes at KLYT I had made our ministry's direction about me and my ideas. But this time I wanted the work to be collaborative, utilizing everyone's talents and gifts to the fullest. I wasn't going to try to get it all done myself; I wanted to be a part of an extremely talented team of people and to help that department be successful.

I approached the opportunity at K-LOVE with a completely different attitude. I knew the new way of doing things was going to be a test for me, but it was also an opportunity—a chance for Living Grace to continue its work.

When we begin to see the world a different way, it is always easier to return to our default lens. But true rebirth takes place when we allow our previous approach to the world to die.

> *"I knew the new way of doing things was going to be a test for me, but it was also an opportunity—a chance for Living Grace to continue its work. When we begin to see the world a different way, it is always easier to return to our default lens. But true rebirth takes place when we allow our previous approach to the world to die."*

My first morning at the station, I remember walking through the hallways of offices and thinking to myself, "I can't believe I'm here." Even though I was thinking about the new job and all that it entailed, I could not help but be entirely absorbed by the moment, the present, the now.

There I was, back in the Christian music industry—a platform and conduit for hope and encouragement that I believed in more than anything else, that I had committed much of my life to, that I deeply loved. And not only was I back in Christian music, but I was at the largest Christian radio network in the world. Though I had seemingly disqualified myself, God had qualified me. Though I had distanced myself from the mere thought of working in Christian radio, God had provided this opportunity for me.

It seems that God wants us to awaken more deeply to how much He loves us.

I WAS BEGINNING TO UNDERSTAND that what mattered most was God's opinion of me, not my own opinion of myself or others' opinions. The story of redemption in my life continued to prevail—even in the darkest corners of my soul, in the areas that I thought were unredeemable.

I had always thought that restoration was about taking something broken and putting it back together. But when God restores something, He restores it to better than what it was before. If I was a car that had been totaled, He had not only put me back together; He had turned me into a brand new car. God is in the business of awe-inducing restoration.

My first day of work at K-LOVE gave me the feeling of hope that I would be there for a long time—at least for as long as I could. I loved the people. The mission. The station. I was excited for the new philanthropy department and what I was going to be a part of. And I *loved* the idea of working for Mike Novak, a man of integrity and passion who was an exemplary leader.

> *"God is in the business of awe-inducing restoration."*

When I returned to my hotel after my first day at K-LOVE/Air1, I sat down and reflected on the day.

And that's when it hit me.

June 6, 2010.

My first day on the campus of K-LOVE.

Exactly ten years *to the day* from when I'd left KLYT.

The Identity of the Beloved

- Does your own opinion of yourself conflict with God's opinion of you? Make a list of adjectives that you associate with yourself.

Make a list of adjectives that God associates with you.

• What would it mean for you to believe that you are loved beyond all measure?

• What would it mean for you to believe that God wants to enter into some of the most difficult things in your life, some of your darkest secrets, and some of your biggest regrets?

• Read Jeremiah 33. What does this passage say about God's restoration of Judah? Do you identify with Judah? If so, how? What are some of the statements of brokenness or promise in this passage that resonate with you? Why?

CHAPTER 24
Labels Are Fables

It was tempting to end this book with the story of my return to Christian radio.

With a happy ending.

With a story that epitomizes redemption and restoration.

But the truth is that it would be insincere for me to end the book in such a fashion.

That's because there are still agonizing, heartbreaking things in my life that I am still hoping that God can redeem. There are things that I am continuing to surrender to Him, things that I am continuing to believe that He is willing to enter into.

One of those things is my family.

It is impossible to adequately describe the negative effects that my actions had on my three daughters. In many ways, it has left scars that will never go away. The repercussions for my actions are still ongoing, and this is why it is a constant battle for me to place my value and worth in Christ.

The mistakes of our pasts often distract us from the hope that we have in Christ for the future.

In the previous chapters, my narrative left off at a place where there was a great relationship with my daughters. But the fallout from the divorce has been like a roller-coaster ride. Currently there are some troubling differences and disagreements about some of the realities within our family. Out of respect for my daughters, I will not go into those details.

To make a long story short, I only have a relationship today with my middle daughter. I have appreciated her relationship and presence in my life so much. I'm thankful for her spirit—her willingness to forgive me and redeem the relationship despite past wounds. I love my daughters with everything within me and have tried to give all I possibly can, but nothing will ever be able to undo the mistakes that I made and my betrayal in my marriage with their mother. It pains me. And it still haunts me daily. I just cannot believe how angry and harsh I was toward them.

There are a lot of things I wish I could go back and do over, but that's not how life is. I still hold out hope for a restored and reconciled relationship with all of my daughters.

Thankfully, though there are still existing hardships with my family, God has blessed me with a wife—a lover, a best friend, a companion—who I dearly love and who has been a rock for me during these challenges.

Not long after I moved to Sacramento, Cathy and I got married. We had a low-key, backyard wedding at Mike Novak's house. We encouraged those who attended to dress casually and wear flip-flops. As Cathy says, it was a "cute, summer wedding." It was an amazing day and a celebration that was once again a reminder of how God was redeeming the broken aspects of my story.

I felt like our lives opened up the day that we decided to say, "I do." I love our marriage. Cathy has been the best addition to my life, and we have moved forward together from our pasts and the hurt in our lives. We don't dwell on old things. We've both been able to see God's grace and mercy in second chances. Because of our previous failed marriages, we've been more generous, more forgiving, more caring, and more loving towards one another. And most importantly, she stands available as a stepmother to my daughters and has forged a good relationship with one of them. I'm hoping for the day of reconciliation with the other two.

I'm thankful that I have a partner today who has loved me and supported me in every facet of my life. Someone to have fun with. Someone who is committed to working together for the good of our marriage. I give all the glory and honor to God. Never would I have thought that my life would change the day I sat next to Cathy in Starbucks. But that seems to be the way God works, doesn't it—gifting His people with beautiful, unexpected situations?

God is a God of second chances. He gave me a second chance at working in contemporary Christian music, and He gave me a second chance at marriage. I hope that one day I will get a second chance with my daughters, too.

By now you know that my story is one of brokenness.

I have a strained relationship with my daughters.

I'm on my second marriage.

I've made a lot of mistakes in my life.

But I also have a hope in Christ for the future and a joy in the present.

And in that sense, this is the *perfect* way to end this book.

Because that is my story.

It is messy, but I pray that it will move more and more toward redemption. My story is a collision of brokenness and hope, of dire mistakes and divine grace.

Nothing epitomizes this collision of brokenness and hope more than what I am doing right now at K-LOVE/Air1....

> *"My story is a collision of brokenness and hope, of dire mistakes and divine grace."*

Earlier I mentioned that one of my passions in life is using my platform as a former athlete to speak to young people and hopefully inspire them to pursue their dreams. I was doing this consistently through our "Change the World" school assemblies program at KLYT, and over the years, I've continued to speak from time to time.

Four years into working for K-LOVE, I was given an opportunity to speak at an FCA chapter at Lincoln High School, a public high school in Lincoln, California, thirty minutes north of Sacramento. When I went to bed the night before my talk, I thought that I knew exactly what I was going to speak about, but then I woke up at four o'clock in the morning with all sorts of ideas swimming in my mind.

I had the idea to create more of a visual demonstration that would resonate with the youth of today—to take sticky notes with different labels written on them and then place them all over my body. Not only did I hope that it would be applicable to them, but it was also a snapshot of my story. Some of the labels others had put on me were related to my football career (Part I): too small, too slow, wrong color, wrong neighborhood, not good enough. Some of the labels that I put on myself were related to my life (Part II): failure, disappointment, unworthy, unredeemable, lost, not good enough. I decided that I would use this visual illustration for the first time later that morning when I spoke at Lincoln High School.

I arrived at the school an hour or so before I was supposed to speak to their FCA chapter at noon, and I met with a young lady named Katie, the student sponsor, who had helped to arrange my talk.

"Katie, is there any chance that I'd be able to meet with the principal?" I asked her.

She arranged a quick meeting, and Katie and I went into the principal's office and started talking to him about my purpose for being there.

"Katie," the principal eventually said, "why don't you and Mr. Rich get on the intercom and invite all the students to come to this?"

This startled me a bit because I was prepared to speak to the school's FCA chapter and talk to them about Jesus. And now the whole school was invited?

Katie got on the intercom and announced: "Former NFL player and Super Bowl XII participant Randy Rich will be speaking at noon in the gymnasium; all are welcome to come."

As we walked to the gymnasium, I said to Katie, "I came prepared to share the gospel with these kids and challenge them in their faith since I was speaking to your FCA group."

"You can still do that, Mr. Rich," she said. "This is all voluntary for the kids."

And so I stood in front of three hundred students (compared to their usual FCA attendance of forty to fifty) with sticky notes covering my body. I talked to them about labels and faith.

I challenged them with this simple question:

What if you were to focus on what God says about you?

Not what someone else says about you.

Not what you think about yourself.

"You are God's favorite child," I told them. "You're a champion. You're a dream-maker. You are smart. Don't dream to become someone; dream because you already *are* someone. It's not about the labels that others put on you or the labels that you put on yourself; it's about what you are and who you are inside."

I then extended an invitation for them to make a profession of faith in front of their peers. That day, in front of the principal and a number of teachers, at least fifty kids were moved enough to make a public proclamation that they wanted to start living a life based in the reality that they're deeply loved by God—not because of what they've done or haven't done, but because of who they already are in Christ.

Not long after I'd spoken at Lincoln, my boss Mike Novak had a conversation with me in which he basically asked, "If you could write your job description, what would it look like?" I told him that, though I loved working with people and overseeing their philanthropy department, I've always had a passion to reach and impact young people. I then shared with Mike the story about my speaking engagement at Lincoln High School. He seemed intrigued and inspired.

Before I was hired at K-LOVE/Air1, Mike and I had engaged in discussions about possibly creating a school assemblies program similar to the "Change the World" program I had helped develop at KLYT years before—a way to impact the youth in communities around the country. Because they had a position open in the philanthropy department that needed to be filled at the time I was hired, we hadn't really talked about it since. But four years into my time at K-LOVE, we realized it might be a good time to explore the idea of a school assemblies program again.

We did some brainstorming and decided that we wanted to create a program that would challenge young people to consider the choices that they are making today and how those choices will impact their lives tomorrow. We then launched a pilot program in North Carolina, which had a tremendous response—enough that it encouraged Mike and K-LOVE's leadership to move forward. We were not only able to raise the money to put the program together; we were able to fund it for the entire year.

We officially launched the program in the fall of 2015. We decided to call it "Air1's Dare to Dream" program. Its foundation was based on this question: *How do the labels that we put on ourselves or the labels that we allow others to put on us cover and destroy the dream—and the power of that dream—that God puts in our hearts?*

Since then, Air1's Dare to Dream program has grown and evolved. Between its genesis in the fall of 2015 and the winter of 2017, a three-semester span, we've conducted 154 assemblies and talked to 72,000 students in eleven different states. We've added two new speakers, and the program is continuing to grow. Not only do we take the program into schools to help children awaken their inherent self-worth; we have also gone into prisons to help inmates believe that they have value and worth, a hope and a future, despite the mistakes that they have made.

I've been told that my story resonates on different levels with different demographics. We craft our presentation differently depending on the information we gather from each administration.

At some schools, I talk about my football career and how I had to constantly remove the labels that others tried to put on me, from high school to the NFL—a sort of underdog story that helps encourage students to pursue the dream in their hearts, not because they are sure to attain that dream, but because they are inherently worthy of pursuing it.

At other schools, I will talk about my troubled family background and the difficulties I experienced growing up in Oildale—a story that helps encourage students that they do not have to be defined by their circumstances or socioeconomic background, that they can make good intentional decisions that will help them to rise above the system that binds them, even though the system was not their fault.

At prisons, I not only talk about my family and socioeconomic background, which is often relatable, but I also share with them the mistakes I made in my life and how I felt as if I had lost everything. Though I never committed a crime, my mistakes in my life made me feel as if I was in my own prison cell of guilt and shame, unable to forgive myself.

One of the most insightful things we have experienced in the program is what people write on the comment cards that we pass out at the end of each talk. We have found these cards to be especially revealing in the schools that we go to. On these cards, students have confessed to cutting themselves, drug addictions, depression, suicide, or family struggles—things that we have been able to turn over to counselors at their schools so that the students can get professional help. One time, a student wrote that he was planning on committing suicide after school, but after sitting through the "Dare to Dream" presentation and listening to the story of one of our speakers, he decided that he had dreams that he wanted to pursue. He said that the talk saved his life.

Communities all over the country are allowing us to come into their schools because they have seen a complete attitude change in their students. It's also important for me to say that I do not believe for a second that we are responsible for having this positive impact. I believe it is God working *through* us to meet others in their needs and their hurts.

I AM BEGINNING TO UNDERSTAND that though I do have regrets in my life, nothing in my life is wasted. God can still use us—and our stories—even when we do not feel worthy to be used. God uses our own brokenness as the antidote to heal other broken people.

This chapter is a fitting way to end the book because what I am doing now with Air1's Dare to Dream program comes from a place of some of my deepest pains in life. Looking back, God did the impossible for a purpose. The purpose was not for me. It was for what God wanted to do in and through me, which is what I am doing today: speaking on junior high and high school campuses all over the country.

It has been a long, difficult road. But it has been a wonderful journey.

I ventured through most of my life believing that I wasn't enough—on a seemingly unending search for approval and affection. Through football. Through sex. Through relationships. Through work.

> *"I am beginning to understand that though I do have regrets in my life, nothing in my life is wasted. God can still use us—and our stories—even when we do not feel worthy to be used. God uses our own brokenness as the antidote to heal other broken people."*

It took hitting rock bottom for me to approach life and faith differently. For me to finally believe that I was enough, simply because of what God said to be true about me. For me to remove the labels.

Isn't it difficult to *really* believe that we are enough?

The world's voices taunt us and tempt us into thinking that we are incomplete or that there is something wrong with us. Our own interior dialogue can sometimes pull us down and feed into this lack of self-worth and respect for our very selves. I like to help bring worth and value to the kids I speak to because their struggle is my own. It is far too easy in this world of labels, comparisons, projections, and rejection to feel as if we are not enough.

But I've chosen to believe in Christ and what He did—that because of God's love, I am forgiven, loved, cherished, and robed in righteousness. That's how God sees me and how God sees you.

A lot of times I don't see myself that way. My flesh will whisper to me, "It's not true." Sometimes I feel like I am far from being God's favorite child. But that's the battle that Paul talks about in his epistle to the Ephesians. It's not against flesh and blood; it's a war that is waged in the minds of men (6:12).

What I realize now is that God is the one who transforms our minds and our thinking. And the more we can awaken to the realities that we are loved beyond all measure and that He is closer to us than we can ever imagine—*with us* in our struggles, our doubts, our suffering, and our occasional self-loathing—the more transformed our minds will become and the more secure we will be.

Don't dream to be someone; dream because you *are* someone. You aren't born a winner; you aren't born a loser; you are born a chooser. Our truest reality is this: we are the beloved sons and daughters of God. May we all begin to see how loved we actually are, how "enough" we've always been. After all, isn't it easier to dream when we know that there is nothing to lose, when we understand that nothing can shake our identity in Christ?

Time and time again in my life, God has demonstrated to me that the good work he began in me will continually be perfected and brought to completion, as it says in Philippians 1:6. God has never given up on me. He will never give up on you. He has created you for a purpose...friendship with Himself, and out of that friendship will create an overflow of your gifts and talents that will benefit the cause of Christ. And no matter what you have done—no matter what mistakes you have made—He can turn your brokenness into a blessing and turn the dark parts of your story into a light.

Wherever you are on your journey, keep in mind that God has things ahead of you. You might not have any idea what that will entail, but I can assure you that if you are holding onto the coattails of the Holy Spirit, it's going to be an exciting ride.

Lastly, let me assure you of this: nothing is wasted in your life. Not even your failures. Not even your sufferings. Not even the difficulties and traumas you'll never be able to understand. That's just how big God is.

God is with us through it all. No situation—no failure, no loss—is too daunting for our God. If we are willing, God can work His power—bringing a deluge of grace, hope, peace, love, and joy—in our deepest wounds.

Whenever you *feel* like you are not enough, know that it is a lie from the pits of hell.

Whenever you *feel* like your life is wasted, confront the lie with truth—that God has a plan for you, that He is perfecting His work in you, and that He is a God of second, third, and multiple chances.

Whenever you begin to believe that you are not loved, remember the lengths that God went to prove His love *for* you, *to* you, *in* you, and *through* you.

You are always enough.

And therefore nothing in your life is *ever* wasted.

God is love.

And therefore you, too, are overflowing with love.

Dare to Dream

- Reflect on the areas in your life that God has redeemed. Allow your mind to move toward gratitude as you celebrate the redemption that God has orchestrated in your life.

- Read Ephesians 2:1–10. Accepting God's grace can help to propel you into a second chance. Why is this? What is it about grace that empowers and strengthens you in your life?

- If you were covered with sticky notes listing labels that others have put on you and labels that you have put on yourself, what would they say? List them.

- What are some labels you wear that run contrary to God's opinion of you?

- Read Philippians 4:11–13. How can God's grace and love—your deep identity as God's child—bring you contentment? How can a foundation of wholeness and security dare you to dream? What is your dream?

Acknowledgments

To my sister, Judy Smith, who keeps our family connected. Judy, thank you for your friendship and support through my many life challenges. You are truly the matriarch of our family.

To my brother Roger, who set the bar high for his siblings by being kind and honest in every aspect of life. Roger, you are a great example of what a Christian should look like.

To my brother Darrell, who was the closest thing I had to a father figure growing up. Darrell, your dedication to following your athletic dreams inspired me at a very young age.

To my brother Raymond, who is one of the most generous people I know. Raymond, I recall you being very patient with the baby of the family—me—when it came to fishing. I will never forget our trip up the Kern River. Your kids are fortunate to have you in their lives.

To my brother Jim, known to me as Floyd. Floyd, you were always a mystery to me as I don't even remember being around you or meeting you until my eighth-grade graduation. Later in my life I came to know you as a fun-loving and caring person—and certainly the best-looking man in the family. I look forward to seeing you again in heaven.

To my dad, Everett. Dad, even though you weren't around much when I was growing up, you taught me the value of a good work ethic—to never leave a job unfinished and to give everything you have. You worked hard to provide for our family.

To my mom, Agnes. Mom, you were the glue that kept our family together. I always saw you as a committed and loving mother who believed her kids could do anything in life. You were always there to demonstrate that support. Thank you for loving us the best way you knew how. I will see you in heaven.

To Stacey, my oldest daughter. Stacey, I know you are a devout wife and mother and trust that you will raise your children to love the Lord with all their hearts. God's blessings are new every morning, and I hope you continue to experience that for the rest of your life. You have been—and will always be—a leader and influence to those around you.

To Kristin, my middle daughter. Kristin, gosh, have we been on a crazy journey. You are the best. I thank you for the never-ending love and forgiveness you possess. You have faced obstacles that no one in your position will ever understand. Your life has been an example of the title of this book. Nothing is wasted in God's economy, and that goes for all the ups and downs this life affords us. God's love covers a multitude, including every wrongdoing and suffering. Live in this love, and raise your children with the same spirit.

To Kelsey, my youngest daughter. Kelsey, I have always admired your sense of loyalty to those who are closest to you. In my opinion, your calm, thoughtful attitude has always produced well-thought-out and careful communication. I love the humor you bring to every gathering and know your children will prosper in that environment.

To my sisters-in-law, brother-in-law, nephews, and nieces. I love you all and appreciate who each of you are.

To the pastors who have influenced me on my Christian journey: Ron Miller, Dan Johnston, Jim Gordon, Skip Heitzig, Jay Kulinna, Dick Woodward, Dr. Charles Stanley, and especially Wayne Barber. I believe that each of you was a mouthpiece of the Lord speaking into my life and influencing my spiritual view of our heavenly Father. I thank each and every one of you.

The Lord has blessed me with so many friends. I wish I could name you all, but I can't. However, I want to offer a special thanks to Bill Nichols, Rick Davis, and Skip Slayton for their lifelong friendship. Most people would be happy to have one friendship last a lifetime. I'm blessed to have three.

To my dear partner, Cathy. You are incredible! When I thank God for second chances, I thank Him most for you. You jumped on board a speedboat when you said yes to me, and you have made so many adjustments to your style of living to accommodate my hectic schedule. I am forever grateful to you, and I love you more each day we are given together.